A NO-NONSENSE GUIDE TO GREEN

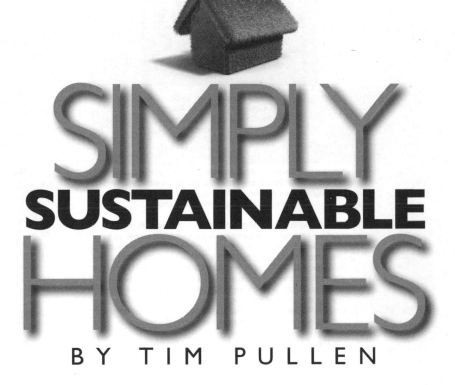

SIMPLY SUSTAINABLE HOMES

BY TIM PULLEN

an **ovolo** book

BUILDING HOMES FOR A CHANGING WORLD

SIMPLY SUSTAINABLE HOMES

Ovolo Publishing Ltd
I The Granary, Brook Farm,
Ellington, Huntingdon,
Cambridgeshire
PE28 0AE

First published 2008

Publisher: Mark Neeter
Design: Gill Lockhart

ISBN: 978-1-905959-044

Printed in the UK by Cromwell Press,
Trowbridge, Wiltshire, UK

For more great Ovolo titles visit:
www.ovolobooks.co.uk

CONTENTS

ACKNOWLEDGMENTS

I want to acknowledge the contributions and help given to me in writing this book. I would like to extend my gratitude to the for all the help, etc. ...

Nicole Jones, Architect of Carmarthen – for her ideas, encouragement and enthusiasm.

Meiron Jones, Architect with Carmarthenshire County Council – for how the idea of sustainability is viewed.

Colin King, Head of Building Research Establishment, Wales – for technical assistance and an insight to the workings of The Code and Ecohomes.

Andrew Teitge MSc, renewable energy consultant and environmentalist – for his technical corrections.

Amanda Pullen, my daughter, for her extensive and invaluable research work.

Monica Margarite Midgley, without who's spelling, grammar and punctuation this book would be incomprehensible.

Picture Acknowledgments

COVER: GETTY IMAGES. DIAGRAMS: BOUNFORD.COM. PAGE 6: WWW.PROVEN ENERGY. PAGE 18 MARK WELSH, WWW.OAKWRIGHTS.CO.UK. PAGE 53: WWW.PROVEN ENERGY. PAGE 64: SEGEN MICROGENERATION, PROVEN ENERGY. PAGE 66: SOLAR CENTURY. PAGE 80: WWW.ORGANICENERGY.CO.UK, WWW.HIGHLANDWOODENERGY.CO.UK, PAGE 100: EVA WARD AT WWW.FINDHORN.ORG, ANDREW LEE. PAGE 115: ADRIAN LAYCOCK LTD, PAGE 127: WWW.COBCOTTAGE.COM. PAGE 127: H&R MAGAZINE, PAGE 135: JEREMY PHILLIPS

ABOUT THE AUTHOR

Tim Pullen is an expert in sustainable building and energy efficiency. He works at green homes consultancy Weather Works (www.weatherworks.co.uk) advising clients on renewable energy and efficiency in the home. Contact: tim@weatherworks.co.uk

CHANGE IS A PROCESS,
NOT AN EVENT.
THE EVENT IS STARTING
THE PROCESS.

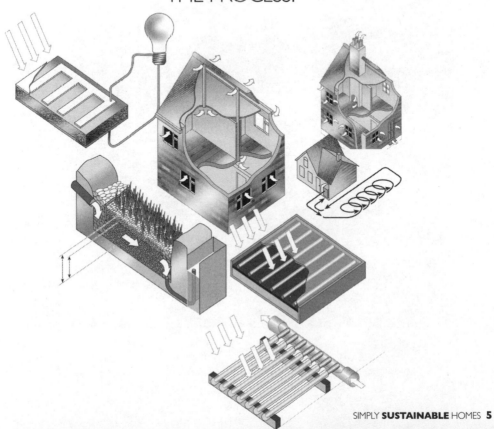

COURTESY PROVEN ENERGY

INTRODUCTION

What we aim to do here is provide a simple guide to anyone wishing to build their own home or upgrade an existing house in a sustainable way. We start from the point that we live in western Europe in the 21st century and have grown used to little luxuries like flush toilets and electric lights. Reverting to a former lifestyle – living like granny – recognises the failings of the way we live, but denies any beneficial advances of the 20th century, and there have been many. My granny lived in an East End slum and as far as I remember, it was neither pleasant nor sustainable.

Having said that, I live in a house built in 1817 which, except for the addition of central heating, double glazing and indoor plumbing, functions in largely the same way as intended by its builder Mr Jonathon Morgan.

As I travel around the country I see many examples of 100-year-old-plus houses that are the same. The biggest problem lies in houses built in the last 60 years. The need for cheap, quick houses post-WW2 followed by the availability of cheap fuel in the form or North Sea oil, led us down the wrong path. It is an extension of the old clichés of a quick fix and the age of disposability.

This book seeks to set out a way for the modern renovator or builder to produce a home that our children, and their children, can live in comfortably and sustainably.

Why would you want to do it? Why would I want you to do it?

We live in an oil-driven economy (literally). Pretty much everything we do, every move we make, is affected by the price of oil. In early 2007, the headlines were **Oil Prices Set To Fall 30 percent!**

In your dreams, would seem to be the appropriate response. The world price of crude oil is around $63 per barrel and pundits are predicting the market is set to fall, bringing the price down to $40 per barrel. You have to ask the question why?

Oil is a finite resource. It will run out and the only question is when. Mr Daniel Clark-

Lowes, managing director of Nubian Consulting, who provides analytical services to the oil industry, tells me that the rate at which we are finding new sources of oils is being outstripped by the increase in demand from developing countries. Demand is increasing faster than supply and if market forces still operate, there may be a short-term fall, but in the long term the price must rise.

In the UK, consumption of oil has risen by a fairly steady 2 percent per year since the 1940s, until 2005, when it appears to plateau. And a similar story can be seen across most of western Europe, which may be why pundits are suggesting a fall in price.

The past three years has seen the price of domestic heating oil rise by some 84percent across the country. Distributors of domestic heating oil are predicting a rise of 20 percent to 30 percent in the next 12 months. It has to be said that history, geology and market laws are all pointing against a significant and lasting fall in oil prices.

That fossil fuels generally, and oil specifically, are contributors to global warming is increasingly becoming accepted. As is the fact that global warming is a reality. In the past five years or so there has been a shift in the position of the global warning deniers. They first denied that global warning was a reality, it did not exist and was all the figment of over-excited imaginations. They then moved to a position of saying that it does exist, but is nothing to do with CO_2 or human intervention; it is a natural phenomenon that will go away in time. They now maintain that it does exist, it is related to CO_2 and human intervention, but there is no point in doing anything while China, India, or anyone far away is building a new coal-fired power station every two weeks.

It is the sort of argument that might more usually be found in the school playground. If we, the people who created the problem, are not prepared to do anything, why should anyone else?

There are possibly four main reasons why you and I should do it:

1. **Money** – if achieving sustainability and zero CO_2 emissions cost no more than staying as we are, there would be no argument. But we are all affected by financial considerations to a greater or lesser extent and achieving those two goals can be expensive. But if we look at the whole- life cost of the house, sustainability, and specifically renewable energy, will always save money. Maybe we need to take a longer-term view and make the investment for our children's sake.

2.   Save the planet – it is difficult to deny that what is good for the planet is good for the individual. Each of us, as we walk across the world, leave a footprint, however small, and the effects of global warming will not be limited to those that cause it. If we, as individuals, are not prepared to act to minimise our footprint then what right do we have to ask others to act? Houses use 27 percent of the UK's energy each year and as a consequence account for 22 percent of the CO_2 emissions. Which actually represents a fall of 2.9 percent since 1999. So what we are doing with sustainable building is beginning to work.

3.   Insurance – specifically using renewable energy as protection against the oil industry. The rate at which we are finding new sources of oil is being outstripped by the increase in demand from developing countries. Demand is increasing faster than supply and if market forces still operate, the price of oil must rise. Which will, of course, in turn affect the price of gas and electricity.

4.   Smugness – or perhaps self-satisfaction would be a better expression. Creating a more sustainable home with lower carbon emissions (and lower running costs) is difficult and an achievement in itself. Kevin McCloud (of Channel 4's *Grand Designs*) said that building your own home is the last great adventure – akin to having a baby or writing a novel. Doing it at all will make you feel good. Doing it sustainably will, quite rightly, make you feel great.

If we act and are wrong and global warming turns out to be just a scare story, the result is that we end up living in better homes. If we do nothing and global warming is a reality, the result is water lapping around our nostrils.

SUSTAINABLE HOMES AND ZERO CARBON

What is the difference between a sustainable home and an eco-friendly home? To begin with, any home cannot be eco friendly by definition. Whatever you build, even an earth shelter, will not have a positive impact on the ecology. The best we can achieve is to reduce the level of unfriendliness.

'Sustainability means meeting our needs today without compromising the ability of future generations to meet their own needs.'

UIA/AIA World Congress of Architects, June 1993

SIMPLY **SUSTAINABLE** HOMES

A sustainable home provides accommodation and facilities for us and future generations in a way that has the lowest possible impact on the ecology and on natural resources. That applies to the build process, the operation of the building and its eventual demolition and/or re-use.

Dealing with the carbon issue, what the Government actually means by 'net zero carbon' is effective carbon dioxide emissions that are equal to – or less than – the actual carbon dioxide emissions. What this allows for is, say, wood-burning boilers. Wood emits CO_2 as it burns, but the amount of CO_2 is no more than was absorbed by the tree when it grew.

Burning fossil fuels (gas, coal or oil either directly or in a power station) produces carbon dioxide (CO_2), which we now all understand to be a major factor in global warming. The word 'net' also means you can buy energy from the electricity grid or mains gas to your heart's content, so long as you put a similar amount of renewable energy back. It is actually aimed at the property developer (Barrett Homes, Wimpey Homes, Bovis Homes, et al.) who develop large estates. It can make better commercial sense for them to use existing mains energy supplies and put up, say, a big wind turbine to off-set the carbon emissions. For the self builder the problem is slightly different if the intended legislation is interpreted to include single property developments. This is looking likely: Carwyn Jones of the Welsh Assembly has stated: 'By 2010 all new buildings will achieve zero carbon emissions.' Clarification sought emphasised that it meant ALL new buildings. The Westminster Government have made a similar statement (although the deadline for England is 2016) then we will be forced to produce 100 percent of the energy needed by the building on site – irrespective of whether the location of the site is conducive to micro-generation. The way the legislation is being framed, it is likely that major renovations and refurbishments will be similarly affected.

As to sustainability, what is meant is a home that minimises its impact on the planet in terms of energy and resources used in its construction, the materials it is built from, and the energy and resources used by the people living in it. And, in that, water is included as a resource.

RENEWABLE ENERGY

Any home claiming sustainability credentials will have to incorporate renewable energy in some form.

There is a lot of talk about wind turbines and heat pumps, most of which is, at best, misleading. Wind turbines in urban locations do not work well, if at all. The managing director of a major wind turbine manufacturer (products available at your local DIY shed) stated in February 2007 that only one in five customers have a suitable site, which is probably optimistic. In urban locations, it is more likely to be one in 1000.

Similarly, heat pumps are becoming big news on the back of advertising that claims reductions in heating bills of 'up to 70 percent'. There are heat pump customers out there whose electricity bills have trebled or even quadrupled as a result of poor designs based on poor information. These disaster situations are not the fault of the technologies but rather of the people selling them.

In almost all circumstances renewable energy is site specific. What will work well in one location will not necessarily work in the next. To look at any renewable-energy technology as you would a gas or oil-fired boiler is always a mistake. They are just not that well understood. If you want a gas condensing boiler your local plumber need only stick his nose in the door to be able to say, with some certainty: 'What you need here is a Galaxy Superstar PDQ123,' and he would be right. Ask him if your ground conditions are suitable for a Kensa 12 kW heat pump and he will suck his teeth, shuffle his feet and tell you to install a gas boiler instead.

Designing in the right renewable energy technology requires a careful consideration of your site, the property you are building or renovating, and the way you live in that property. It is second in importance only to designing in the right insulation. There is no magic about it. The right system will work well. The wrong system poorly installed will not work and will cost you a lot of money.

FINANCIAL IMPLICATIONS

Building a sustainable home is more expensive than putting up a non-sustainable alternative. But achieving a reasonable level of sustainability need not cost significantly more. It should also be recognised that many aspects of sustainability have been falling in price in recent years, most notably renewable energy.

Sustainable homes are beginning to command a premium price, which has been shown in developments from Tyne & Wear to Cornwall. It is demonstrated by developers successfully selling 'sustainable' homes at premium prices that actually have very thin sustainable credentials. People want to buy sustainable homes and currently it is a seller's market.

Many smaller property developers are opting to build sustainable homes because the premium they attract is far more than the extra cost of development. It may also be good for their image.

SET TARGETS AND ACHIEVE THEM

Any movement towards sustainability is a movement in the right direction, so don't beat yourself up over how far to go. Each of us has different motives, different constraints, different fears and desires. Setting a low target and hitting it is likely to lead to learning and success. Setting a high target and missing could lead to the abandonment of the whole idea. We start from the premise that 100 percent sustainability is not possible. We have to accept that copper pipe, cables, light fittings, plug sockets etc. are more or less unsustainable (although potentially recyclable) and move on from that.

NEW BUILD

Setting targets for a sustainable build will be largely governed by your budget and the amount of effort you can put into finding materials and skilled people. The current legislation (see Appendix 1) will obviously have an effect, but how you achieve what the legislation requires will be largely up to you. As a one-time house builder I know that budgets tend to overrun. I always told clients to allow for at least a 20 percent overrun and was universally ignored – but nonetheless right. With the current state of the sustainable materials market the overrun is likely to be even higher.

There are some areas of the build that are easy. Any home purporting to have sustainable credentials will use a lot of timber – with that timber coming from a sustainable source. Sustainable timber has the lowest embodied CO_2 and has no impact on natural resources.

At the other end of the scale, using limecrete (rather than concrete) for the slab can be expensive, difficult to find and take weeks rather than days to lay. It is the sort of area destined to create a huge budget overrun.

Sustainability is still largely about doing your own research. You will need to find out for yourself what is available in your area. The answer is to consult with your architect, and any other experts in your team, and select specific areas of the property that lend themselves to the use of sustainable materials and methods. Get them properly costed and allow for the 'buggeration' factor in the project plan!

Any substantial building project is stressful. Don't make it more so by setting yourself unachievable targets.

RENOVATION

According to the DTI, 70 percent of the housing stock that will exist by 2050 has already been built. That means that there are a huge number of houses that do not meet current standards for sustainability, CO_2 emissions and energy use. This gives plenty of scope for improvement.

Simple things like insulation and draught proofing are relatively inexpensive and highly effective. If you are planning a major refurbishment or renovation you will be affected by the same legislation as applies to a new build.

THE STANDARD FOUR-BEDROOM/FOUR-PERSON HOUSE AS A COST COMPARATOR

Throughout this book we will be referring to the 'standard house' and drawing comparisons based on that typical size. By the 'standard house,' we are taking a 200m² floor area property, slightly larger than the average house, which is about 130m² to 140m². It will be on two floors, with four bedrooms, 2.5 bathrooms, and four people in occupancy, with a typical work/school occupancy pattern.

Construction (for comparison purposes – not because it is a good idea) will be:

The property will be on a tenth of an acre plot with the rear of the house having a south-facing aspect. Patio doors to the rear give access to the lounge and construction will be block inner skin, brick outer skin, under concrete roof tiles. Part L standard levels of insulation throughout. Solid concrete slab ground floor, with suspended timber first floor with chipboard flooring. Glazing will be uPVC double glazed with 15mm air gap. The house will have a conventional gas condensing boiler with standard pressed steel radiators. Mid-range kitchen and bathroom fittings with tiled floors and tiling to walls. Other floor coverings to be carpet. Gardens to the property will be laid to lawns with flower borders. A driveway of some 15m length to be hard paved, leading to a double garage.

Your house will obviously be different but hopefully you can 'scale off' from this standard.

1 DESIGN RIGHT

A good product starts with a good design. A conventional house can almost take a design off the shelf as, beyond shape, style and size there is little to consider. However, a sustainable home needs more thought. To be sustainable means able to be kept in existence, to be maintainable, to endure. A sustainable home goes further even than that.

If we accept that statement as a guide to what designing a sustainable house means, it leads us to two conclusions:

1. We need to minimise our use of natural resources – that is, materials used in the construction of the house and fuel used in its operation.

2. We need to design houses that can be adapted to meet future needs and/or can be recycled when they are demolished.

The average UK house uses around 200 tonnes of materials in its construction. Of that, 164 tonnes is virgin material (never before used), 12 tonnes is material from industrial waste and 24 tonnes is recycled material (figures from Building Research Establishment (BRE)).

In addition, on average 13 percent of that virgin material will not be used in the property but is defined as accidental waste – broken, lost, off-cuts, etc – that goes straight to landfill. That is 21.3 tonnes of new materials lost, at a cost to the builder estimated at between £3,600 and £4,500.

The average family home of 130m^2 will use around 1,040,000kWh of energy in its life (assuming a life of 80 years). That equates to around 450 tonnes of CO_2 emissions – per house, and there are some 25 million houses in the UK. The Government suggest an immediate reduction of 20 percent in CO_2 emissions from 2005 levels, and an overall reduction to zero by 2016. With those figures you can see why.

DESIGN CRITERIA

The design issues for a sustainable build are largely the same as for a conventional build. The major difference is that they will be brought into sharper focus. The three key factors are identical for both conventional and sustainable build, in order of priority: noise attenuation, ventilation and lighting.

As the owner/builder, you will be making decisions around open plan living or private space. Is the kitchen the hub of the house? Do you need a boot room or mud room by the back door, or maybe a shower room? Do you need to consider cats and dogs sharing your space? What are the circulation issues – is the dining room used daily or for special occasions? Do you need the potential to extend the property as a whole, extending the living areas into the garden or for a granny annex?

All these issues will be discussed with the architect and will influence and be influenced by the materials to be used, the heating and lighting requirements and the construction method to be used.

Sustainability is about finding materials appropriate to the design as locally as possible. If the material, and the skill to use it, can't be found locally, it may be best to leave that area of the project to conventional methods.

It has to be recognised that the level of success will be a product of the amount of effort put in. Sustainable building is still a concept in its infancy. Architects, engineers, builders, tradesmen, builders' merchants all tend towards the conventional, because it is safe. It leaves them in their comfort zone. Building sustainably means getting outside that zone. It means finding new design ideas, new materials, new sources of material, new ways of working with that material. It requires thought and effort and it can be a bit scary.

The answer is to get people on board who either know and understand sustainable construction or who are keen to learn.

SIZE

Above all things, size matters. Put simply, the bigger it is the more material it consumes, the more energy and CO_2 it embodies and the more fuel it takes to run.

The average UK home is 104m^2 , compared to 105m^2 in France and 109m^2 in Germany. The average UK family home is 130m^2 , which compares to just 85m^2 in 1950. A 53 percent increase in size (and consequently materials and energy) in 57 years. This is probably a reflection of the increasing wealth of the nation and we use the house more than anything

1

else to make a statement about our personal wealth and status. Size has become the principal method of measurement.

A method of gauging a build budget is by the cost per square metre (m^2). It will vary with the quality of finishing, the location and the construction method and will currently be something around £500 per m^2 to £1,200 per m^2. The temptation is to start with the overall budget, say £200K and swiftly arrive at the conclusion that a mid-range level of finishing will allow a house of, say, 250m^2 . The question is, does a warm, welcoming, functional, strikingly designed house that makes clever use of space and is efficient in its use of fuel but only 150m^2 say less about the owners than a conventional home of 250m^2? Maybe the answer is to use the same budget but spend a higher proportion on design and sustainable construction.

LOCATION

The location of the property will be driven by a range of personal factors, from where you want to live (region of the country, rural, urban, sub-urban) to proximity to schools, shops, road and rail networks. In sustainability terms, all these issues have a role to play.

A brown-field site has obvious ecological advantages over a green-field site, but may not be in the preferred area. Proximity to essential services and communications links have the potential to reduce car use, but may deny the attraction of a rural location.

Location will also be driven by availability, finding the right plot is not easy and there is often a compromise to be made. It is such a personal issue that it is probably sufficient to know that there are sustainability issues around it. The choice of location will be a factor in the level of sustainability being aimed at.

ORIENTATION

There are two main orientation factors to consider; external, that is, the compass orientation of the building, and internal, the location of the rooms within the building.

In renovation projects it is a matter of working with the existing external orientation, but there may be some potential to alter the internal orientation.

Providing a south-facing elevation and a south-facing roof plane enables access to solar power in all its forms: solar panels, passive solar heat gain and more natural light. It is equally important to arrange the room layout to suit — circulation rooms (living room, kitchen etc) on the south and operational rooms (utility room,

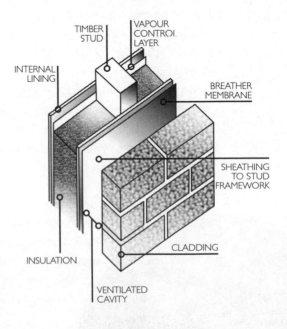

garage, bathrooms) on the north.

This allows the circulation rooms to have large, tall windows that allow in plenty of natural light (tall windows get more light to the back of the room) and operational rooms to have small windows (less heat loss).

Locating a conservatory on the south will significantly increase the solar heat gain, but needs to be designed in properly to allow that heat to disperse through the house or it will over-heat in summer and be too cold in winter.

Rooms with windows on the east are useful as bedrooms, benefiting from morning sun, but living rooms with west-facing windows will be affected by glare from the low setting sun – but will get a good view of the sunset.

Proximity of trees to windows can provide shading which can be beneficial if they are deciduous trees in front of south-facing windows by providing summer shading and winter sun, but detrimental if they are evergreen or in front of east-facing windows.

Orientation also needs to fit in with the topography of the site to take advantage of views and, so far as possible, keep road, rail or other noise as far away as possible and to provide access to the outside space.

Orientation can make or break the comfort and the sense of well-being in the home. Ultimately, orientation will determine how you live in the house.

CONSTRUCTION METHOD

There are two basic construction methods: 'light and tight', which is usually timber frame with maximum insulation and minimum air permeability; or 'mass and glass', which is masonry walls and floors with lots of glass to enable high levels of solar heat to be absorbed. Mass and glass does not preclude high levels of insulation or automatically mean more air leakage.

We are being forced down the light/tight road by Building Regulations requirement to meet an increasingly stringent air-tightness standard, whether we want to or not and whether it is a good idea or not.

TIMBER STUD

VAPOUR CONTROL LAYER

INTERNAL LINING

BREATHER MEMBRANE

SHEATHING TO STUD FRAMEWORK

CLADDING

INSULATION

VENTILATED CAVITY

SIMPLY **SUSTAINABLE** HOMES

1

Left: typical timber-frame construction method. Right: Post and beam construction also gives more flexibility with the room layout, as none of the internal walls will be load bearing.

In terms of sustainability, timber frame carries the best credentials, especially if the timber is from a sustainable source and has sustainable insulation.

The illustration above shows a typical timber-frame construction method, but is it the right way round? Consider the effect of having the masonry cladding on the inside. The structural stability would not be changed, nor would the thermal performance or the permeability. The affect of having the masonry on the inside would be to provide a thermal mass able to absorb and release heat and thereby reduce the amount of energy put into the house. External weather-proofing is still needed, but it doesn't have to be brick or block and render.

Solar heat, that is free heat, is of little value in a house that does not have the thermal mass to absorb it. In a light-weight, air-tight house solar heat presents a problem in terms of how to get rid of it.

Post and beam construction is making something of a resurgence. It is the oldest known form of construction, dating from pre-Grecian times and was for centuries the standard form throughout England. An independently stable structure is constructed with the arrangement of posts and beams, allowing the spaces between to be filled with any suitable material. The image on the right shows clearly the post and beam arrangement, infilled in this case with a glass elevation. It could just as well be timber cladding with an insulation fill of perhaps 200mm. The image on the left is the same principle in a somewhat older building where the panels are infilled with stone and lime render.

Post and beam construction also gives more flexibility with the room layout, as none of the internal walls will be load bearing.

Designing a sustainable home is about challenging the conventions. It is about asking if the methods and materials used are actually the best option available, or are they just being used because it is the way we have always done it? It is often a matter of determining which of construction method and design is the cart and which the horse.

QUALITY OF LIFE

Dealing effectively with noise, daylight, views of the sky, easy access to outside space and good ventilation will improve the comfort of the house and the quality of the lives of the people in it.

Noise is the biggest potential nuisance to any home owner, with the greatest potential to cause discomfort and annoyance. Limiting adverse noise, both incoming and outgoing, has an obvious benefit. It has been shown that allowing daylight into the house without glare and providing views of the sky improves the sense of well-being for the occupants. Similarly good ventilation, natural or mechanical, improves oxygen levels and prevents a damp, musty atmosphere, again improving the sense of well-being. Ventilation has also been recognised as a factor in sick-building syndrome.

None of these issues are difficult to deal with at the design stage, but can be impossible to deal with later. There is a balance between light and glare, light and solar heat gain, ventilation and draughts. Get the balance wrong and at best there is an on cost to rectify the situation and at worst the house is difficult to live in.

SOLAR HEAT

Solar heat is free heat. It falls on every house, but is seldom used to its full potential.
To calculate the amount of heat produced by a south-facing window, multiple the area of the window in m² by 868 and divide the answer by 3.4 for a result in watts.

For example:
A room with a 4m² patio door and a 1.6m² window on the south elevation of a room with a floor area of 20m²
Heat gain in watts: 5.6m² x 868 divide by 3.4 = 1429 watts

The acceptable level of solar heat gain is 25w per m² of floor area. In this case, a 20m² floor area room will be receiving 71.5w per m². It will therefore need some cooling in summer and there are four ways of dealing with it:

1

1.   Mechanical cooling, for example, air conditioning
2.   Retractable blinds to provide shading
3.   Planting – trees or other plants to provide shading
4.   Open the patio doors

Obviously designing a room that will require air conditioning does not fall within the sustainable remit.

Retractable blinds fitted over the window and patio door provide an acceptable and effective solution, but they add cost and increase the embodied CO_2 of the house.

Planting deciduous trees in front of the south elevation (poplar, plane or similar) will provide dappled shade in summer and allow sunlight though in winter. Although poplars have a high growth rate, there may still be a short-term issue with shading until the trees are up to height.

An alternative may be to plant clematis or similar on a pergola-type structure outside the patio doors. This will not only provide adequate shading, but will also encourage greater use of the outside space.

NATURAL VENTILATION

We are being forced down a road of air-tightness by building regulations that will make mechanical ventilation a necessity. But there is still an argument for natural ventilation and specifically in relation to passive solar heat and encouraging it to move through the building with passive ventilation.

Natural ventilation used to be a matter of opening the window, trickle vents and air brick but has moved on a bit from there. Thermostatic window actuators (electric opening when the room gets too hot) are becoming more trendy, as are passive roof cowls – either the old middle-eastern wind towers that push air down into the building or cowls that use the wind to draw air from the building. All these systems provide a fair degree of control over the amount of air moving through the building and the direction of its movement, either mechanically through dampers or electronically. They also use little or no energy to do it.

Simply opening the windows can achieve the same thing, but with a good deal less control. If windows are to be used then it is necessary to design the right openings in the right places to achieve proper ventilation.

Horizontal pivot openings offer the best ventilation capability as they tend to be effective in any wind direction. Vertical pivot openings work well as air scoops when the wind direction is parallel to the wall, but need articulation to the building elevation (eg bay windows) to create a local pressure difference.

With any of the natural ventilation options, a good understanding of the systems, heating and ventilating, and the design issues around them is essential. As we move towards ever more air-tight buildings the issue of ventilation becomes increasingly important. The old rule of 5 percent of floor area as opening windows no longer applies and it is no longer something that can be left to guesswork or luck. Air-tightness beyond 7m³/hr needs the expert advice of a heating and ventilation engineer to ensure safety and health. See Assembling the Right Team, this section.

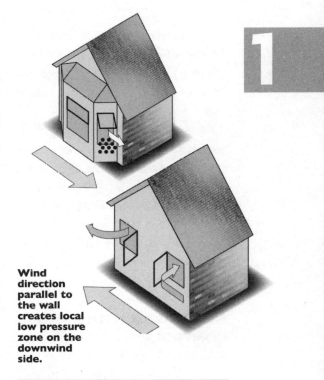

Wind direction parallel to the wall creates local low pressure zone on the downwind side.

ENERGY USE

We are required by building regulations to provide a SAP rating (Standard Assessment Procedure) at the design stage of the project. The SAP calculation will come up with a figure of up to 100. It may be 64, 82, 47, but unfortunately very few of us know what that figure means. We know that a high figure is good and a low figure is bad, but it takes a detailed examination of the SAP calculation to find out how much energy the building will actually use.

The SAP calculation will give a figure in kWh per year which needs to be divided by the total floor area. We are looking for a figure of less than 100kWh/m² to comply with 2005 Building Regulations insulation standards. A property looking for sustainability credentials will want to go some way past this figure and 75kWh/m² should be comfortably achievable.

The point of this is two fold: the figure relates directly to the amount of fuel the property will consume and what it will cost to run; if some or all of that fuel is fossil fuel, the figure also translates into CO_2 emissions.

1

Our standard house, conventionally insulated will emit a total of 5.94 tonnes of CO_2 every year. As a point of interest, one tonne of CO_2 is enough to fill a balloon 10m in diameter.

Taking the energy efficiency rating of the home is still something of a new idea, we are usually more interested in the sale value. It is only in the last year or two that energy use and running cost have come into the equation at all. A sustainable home will put energy use at the heart of the design process. Not only the amount of energy used, but also the source of that energy.

CONVERT KWH TO CO²:

For natural gas multiply by 0.19
For oil multiply by 0.25
For grid electricity multiply by 0.43

So our standard house of 200m² will use 20,000kWh of natural gas heating and 5,000kWh of electricity each year. That is;

Gas - 20,000 x 0.19 = 3800kg or 3.80 tonnes
Electricity - 5,000 x 0.43 = 2150kg or 2.14 tonnes

HEATING, LIGHTING AND CONTROLS

In a house built to 2005 Building Regulations standards, 77 percent of the energy used in the building will go to space and water heating and 23 percent to power – lighting, TV, computer, etc.

There is a strong focus on reducing the electricity used for lighting in the home. It is a good idea, it is easy to do, it does have an immediate impact (changing a 100w bulb to a low-energy equivalent will save £8 per year), but it is a bit of a soft target. Lighting uses just 3 percent of the energy in the home. The same as consumer electronics, cooking and only slightly more than wet appliances.

The big energy user is space heating, accounting for up to 60 percent of the total. A good control system could reduce the energy bill by 15 percent, will cost perhaps £300 (if installed with a new heating system) and will allow different temperatures and different heating times

1

for each room or each zone of the house. Why heat a bedroom from 5:00pm when there is no intention to use it until 11pm? Why heat a guest bedroom to the same temperature as other bedrooms when it is not going to be used at all?

Designing the right systems for heating, lighting and ventilation is critical, but having control over those systems is the only way to make sure they work efficiently. Provision to install those control system is ideally made at the design stage.

MATERIALS

A pre-determination for a particular material will go a long way towards determining the overall design. For example, the client who wants a turf roof will strongly influence everything that goes under it. A pre-disposition for ship-lap cladding will make the decision for straight walls as ship-lap does not do curves well.

In terms of sustainability the only essential prerequisite is that as many materials as practically possible should be from sustainable sources.

Unless the architect and/or builder are particularly enthusiastic, the use of recycled or reclaimed materials will be limited to those that the client finds. Local research of architectural salvage yards and demolition yards can be extremely revealing. From mundane roof slates to the more esoteric – interesting wall or floor tiles – it is truly amazing what can be found with a little effort. Just knowing what is potentially available will help in the decision making process and may open up whole new lines of thought.

The scope of the sustainable materials available will be largely a product of the research and effort that the client puts in. Listed below are just some of the many websites selling sustainable materials.

www.rounded-developments.org.uk
www.greenconsumerguide.com
www.greenshop.co.uk
www.aecb.net

Timber will always be a big part of any sustainable build so check out the Forestry Stewardship Council and www.fsc.org to make sure that the timber you buy is from a sustainable source.

1

WATER

Did you know that the average household (four people) uses 175,000 litres of water each year, and that each litre needs 0.05kWh of energy to get it to the tap? That is 876kWh of energy to deliver drinking quality water to each house.

Did you also know that up to 35 percent of that high quality water, and energy, goes straight down the toilet?

Toilets use, on average, 61,000 litres of water per year. A low-flush cistern will reduce that to 40,000. An ultra-low-flush to under 30,000 litres.

Showers use, on average, 35,000 litres per year. An aerated shower head reduces the quantity of water used to around 17,000 litres.

The same story is true of taps, dishwashers and washing machines. How far anyone goes in terms of saving water is a matter of personal choice and it has to be considered that grey water or rainwater harvesting systems will take a long time to recover their cost in terms of reduced water bills. A rainwater harvesting system will cost around £3,000 installed, but against that needs to be stacked the convenience of having a water supply that is free of any energy input, available to water the garden or wash the car and not subject to hose-pipe bans.

SURFACE TREATMENTS

As with most elements of the house, the perceived wisdom of asphalt drives and concrete patios is not the only option. Water permeable alternatives are available for all external surface treatments. These options have three benefits:

1. They reduce the rainwater run-off to drains reducing the risk of overloading the drainage system and of flash flooding.
2. They allow more water back into the water table, making it available for extraction as drinking water.
3. They challenge the way we look at external surfaces to provide potentially more aesthetically-pleasing treatments.
4. They improve the local ecology.

WASTE AND RECYCLING

In terms of the operation of the house, it is simply a matter of providing adequate space for the separation of waste into recyclable stores. Certainly internally, but perhaps externally as well with the provision of composting bins.

In terms of construction, remember that some 21 tonnes of waste (to say nothing of excavation spoil) will be produced during the build project. A trial conducted by two major house builders found that sorting and separating this waste reduced the build cost by an average 8 percent. Costs were saved in two ways: materials were recovered and reused, haulage and landfill charges were reduced.

It makes obvious commercial sense as well as environmental sense to consider what actually is rubbish.

SHAPE AND STYLE

If we are using the opportunity of a sustainable build to limit the area of the internal space, clever use of that space will influence the shape and style of the property. Softening the boundaries between inside and the outside and encouraging the use of the outside as a living space will go some way towards 'bringing the garden into the home'.

The shape and style of the property will always be an issue personal to the owners and there are two ways of dealing with it:

1. The client takes their preconceived ideas of shape and style to the architect, whose job then is little more than to produce plans that will obtain planning consent and meet Building Regs requirements.

2. The client sets out a remit for the architect, providing their preferences and thoughts around all the issues listed above. The architect then is allowed to use their creative and technical skill to design a property to suit the client's remit and lifestyle.

The decision as to which option to take will be influenced by the quality of the architect, so many of whom are middle-aged men, locked into a methodology that has served them throughout a 30-year career.

The shape and style of the building will influence, and be influenced by, the construction

1

method and materials. Deciding a construction method or type of material early on will pre-determine, or at least constrain, the shape and style of the building. And exactly the reverse applies as well. Clients who pre-select the shape and style of building they want are in danger of restricting the architect's creativity, turning them into a simple draftsman and technician, and limiting their options for new materials and construction methods.

Shape and style is a function of all the above criteria. It is also a function of the landscape in which the building sits. A good design will take all those considerations into account and a good design needs a good designer.

ASSEMBLING THE RIGHT TEAM

A good architect will be central to any successful project, sustainable or conventional. The relationship between architect and client is a very close and personal one and time spent researching your architect and finding one that has the same enthusiasm for sustainability, and speaks the same language as you do, will be time well spent.

A good architect will also know their own limitations and the experts needed to fill the gaps. As a minimum, that is likely to be a structural engineer and quite possibly a heating and ventilation engineer. The project will also need a builder, and maybe a lighting engineer, a project manager and an interior designer. They, too, must have proper knowledge of, or the enthusiasm to learn about, sustainability and renewable energy.

Most clients consider themselves adequately qualified project managers, interior designers and lighting engineers, but is that really the case? As an instance, the interior designer needs to be more than a make-over artist. They need to be able to help with use of light, flows around living spaces, juxtaposition of one room to another as well as the more usual things like colour, texture and mood. All these things may be within the architect's capability but are they really within the capability of the untrained client? The client wants, above all things, a successful project and to achieve that they have a responsibility to recognise their own limitations, just as the professionals they engage do.

There is an old Native American saying: 'If you want to go quickly, go alone. If you want to go far, go together.' Building a sustainable home is not a sprint and you will achieve more, go further, in company with others.

UNDERSTANDING YOUR HOUSE AS A MACHINE

As part of the design team, a critical part in as much as they are the decision-maker, the client will build a good understanding of how the house is designed to operate.

The usual example is that if the house is designed to be air tight, don't open the windows. But obviously it goes much further than that. A house is a large, complex machine with many issues relating to its performance, maintenance and efficiency. Both Ecohomes and The Code for Sustainable Homes require that a manual be produced to set out all those issues on paper, recognising the importance of understanding the house and how it was designed to be run.

2 THE UNSEXY

L et's be clear, the greatest environmental impact of a house is from the fossil fuels it burns for its energy. No amount of eco-certified, recycled bamboo flooring can compensate for the impact of a gas-guzzling house. Conserving energy, minimising the energy needs of the house, has to be the first priority.

In short, insulation is king. The money invested in insulation will go on repaying for the whole life of the building. Not only in financial terms but also in terms of its CO_2 emissions. And if it is sustainable insulation, it will have minimal impact on natural resources and can be recycled into the next house.

Energy conservation does not start and end with insulation. There is also lifestyle and construction to consider. The Government tell us almost daily that switching off lights, TVs, phone chargers and turning the thermostat down a couple of degrees will save 20 percent on the fuel bill. And they are right. How you live in your house is still a matter of personal choice, but increasingly how you build your house is being dictated by Government policy and the Building Regulations.

AIR TIGHTNESS

It is mandatory for all houses gaining planning consent after April 2006 to meet the Building Regulations Part L1 A standard on air tightness. That standard is a 'leakage' of not more than $10m^3/h/m^2$@50Pa. That is, 10 cubic metres of air per hour escaping for every square metre of the envelope surface area with the air at a pressure of 50 Pascals. What that actually means is a bit of a mystery and whether it is a good idea is another thing altogether. We are being forced to adopt air-tightness standard, but not being told that without mechanical ventilation, dehumidification and effectively air conditioning, we will be living in a warm, damp, foul-smelling atmosphere polluted with the chemicals gassed-off from construction materials. That atmosphere will be the ideal

breeding ground for every kind of fungus, mould, dust mite, bacteria and virus. What that will lead to in health terms needs a different kind of expert, but it can't be good.

The 2005 building regulations stated that we had to have a maximum of 1.5 air changes per hour (ach). It was in the late 1980s that the standard changed from a minimum to a maximum. Until 2005, 1.5ach was considered to be the minimum amount of air needed to maintain oxygen levels, clear out exhalation CO_2, pollutants and smells. The 2006 regulations are based, at least in part, on the Canadian R2000 standard which calls for 0.8ach at 50pa.

When asked why 10m³ was chosen as the standard, Mr Colin King, head of BRE Wales, who was influential in drafting the standard, said: 'It is an arbitrary figure. It has no direct relationship to air changes per hour.' But, of course, there has to be a relationship and the 10m3 standard is said to be around 1.2ach. And to put that in perspective, the German Passiv Haus standard calls for 'less than 1ach' but again at 50pa.

The change comes as a result of a Government fact finding mission to Canada and Sweden in 2002 to figure out how to make our houses more energy efficient. They came back with the clear idea that controllability was the answer. What we had was uncontrolled air movement through trickle vents and air bricks, and what Canada and northern Europe had was air movement controlled by mechanical ventilation. The model for our new standard was Canada's R2000 E-House, which also mandates that mechanical ventilation is a requirement in all new homes. It recognises that with less than 1.5ach there is a build up of pollutants and CO_2 that become unpleasant and possibly damaging to health. An air tightness of 0.6ach provides a background air change rate that provides just 42 percent of the air required to provide enough oxygen to breathe.

At 10m³/h (or 1.2ach) it is possible that the building will be 25 percent more energy efficient than the 2005 standard. If we achieve the target standard of 5m³/h BRE say that we will save 40 percent of the heating energy consumption. To make the standard work we need two things: a house that remains sealed, and a reliable mechanical ventilation system. To not put too fine a point on it, with permeability at even 5m³/h, if the ventilation system breaks down there is a good chance of suffocating. Which is why the Canadian standard mandates for ventilation systems and that they must be connected to mains electricity.

At a meeting of the Energy Efficiency Working Group at the Department for Communities and Local Government on May 5, 2006, the minutes show that the target permeability is actually 3m³/h/m²@50pa. But there is a problem. To quote: '7m³/h would be good but let's get 10m³/h first. Testing is still being ignored by many local authority building control officers.' It goes on to say that the standard will be increased to 5m³/h and eventually 3m³/h but that 'the building industry just will not stand for it yet.' Which begs the question why not? If it

2

saves 40 percent+ of the energy consumption and similarly reduces running costs, surely buyers would be queuing up for these massively energy efficient houses?

The Canadian standard is based, quite reasonably, on the requirements of the Canadian climate. They have winters of -20^{0}C and summers of +25^{0}C and those temperatures will hold for months every year. That is not the British experience. In addition, those Canadian temperatures lead to a dry climate (moisture gets frozen out of the air in the long cold winters, and burnt out in the summer). So much so that the mechanical ventilation systems inject moisture into the air to prevent excessive drying in the house. Again, not the British experience. In fact, our problem will be the reverse. To quote Mr Colin King again: 'It is a matter of education. It is a lifestyle change. People will have to learn to not open their windows and not dry clothes indoors. Just as they learnt not to bung up trickle vents with tissue paper because they felt a draught.'

What happens to those potential energy savings if we don't absorb the education, or choose not to change our lifestyle? If we live in the hermetically sealed houses now demanded in the same way as we do in our current draughty properties, the energy savings literally go out the window. The Department of Communities and Local Government figures imply that without the necessary lifestyle change our energy consumption will actually increase. The heating systems will be running flat out to keep up with the open windows, added to which will be the mechanical ventilation that will be trying to dehumidify all that incoming air.

It would seem to be something more than tissue paper in trickle vents. It would seem to be a matter of culture and habit – lifestyle, as Mr King said. We have a habit of enjoying the fresh air, of opening windows and moving freely in and out of the house without having to pass through a double-door air lock. That habit has developed because we live in a temperate, relatively damp climate, not the icy extremes of Canada and Northern Europe. Whether the necessary lifestyle changes will be adopted or not is a moot point. I, for one, would not be happy if I could not open the windows and listen to the birdsong while I sit at my desk writing and thinking.

Typical heat loss U-values and proportions through fabric

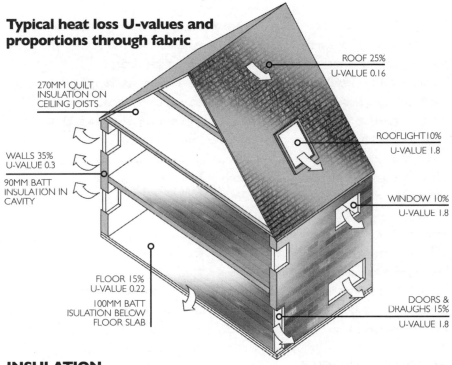

ROOF 25%
U-VALUE 0.16

270MM QUILT INSULATION ON CEILING JOISTS

ROOFLIGHT 10%
U-VALUE 1.8

WALLS 35%
U-VALUE 0.3

90MM BATT INSULATION IN CAVITY

WINDOW 10%
U-VALUE 1.8

FLOOR 15%
U-VALUE 0.22

100MM BATT ISULATION BELOW FLOOR SLAB

DOORS & DRAUGHS 15%
U-VALUE 1.8

INSULATION

The speed with which heat escapes from a building is measured by its thermal resistance – the more insulation, the more resistance. To calculate a specific U-value use one of the free calculators available on the web. A good and simple-to-use one is available from Build Desk at www.builddesk.co.uk It is free to download and will calculate U-values for most common building materials.

U-values are expressed in $W/m^2/{}^0C$, which is watts per square metre per degree Centigrade (sometimes degrees Kelvin or K is used, but it is exactly the same). What that means is that the lower the figure the fewer Watts of heat are escaping through that material. Part L Building Regulations 2006 set a minimum standard for U-values of :

PART L 2006 – U-Values

Walls	0.30	Pitched roof – insul at rafter	0.20
Floors	0.22	Windows etc.	1.80
Flat roof	0.20	Doors >50% glass	2.20
Pitched roof – insul at ceiling	0.16	Other doors	3.00

2

To achieve these U-values needs 90mm of high density foam (Celotex, Kingspan or similar) in the walls, 100mm polystyrene in the floor, 270mm quilt insulation in the roof and Low-E double glazing with 15mm gas-filled gap for windows and glazed doors.

If you install these levels of insulation your heating load will be around 100kWh per square meter of floor area per year. So our standard house will, in very broad terms, use 20,000 kWh of space heating per year. An oil-fired condensing boiler will use about 2,000 litres of oil to generate that heat at a cost of £700 (at 35p per litre).

By comparison, 2002 Part L required U-values of :	
Walls	0.35
Floors	0.25
Pitched roof	0.35
Windows etc.	2.2

The heat loss will be almost 50 percent higher as will the cost of heating. The cost of the extra insulation needed to achieve the 2007 levels would be recovered in less than three years.

THERMAL BRIDGING

A study for the US Army in 2005 showed that a 4 percent gap in the insulation (of a highly insulated building) accounted for 50 percent of the heat loss. It is the basis of the reasoning for the air-tight house and shows that if the insulation is not installed properly a good deal of its benefit is lost. Heat will find the line of least resistance in its struggle to flee the building, and thermal bridges are a good means of escape.

A thermal bridge is typically found where vertical and horizontal layers of insulation meet but don't overlap.

If you can draw a straight line from the interior of the property to the exterior without passing through a full thickness of insulation, you have a thermal bridge. They are very tricky to deal with in a retro-fit or renovation as access to the problem area is usually a problem. They tend to occur over windows and doors, at the junction of the walls and roof and at the junction of the ground floor and walls.

In a new build, they are easily dealt with at the design stage, so long as you look for them.

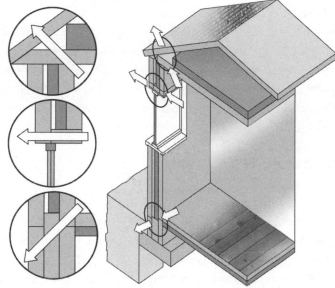

2

A thermal bridge is a straight line drawn from the interior to the exterior that does not pass through a full thickness of insulation

INSULATION MATERIALS

NON-SUSTAINABLE MATERIALS

The non-sustainable market is covered by four market leaders; Kingspan, Celotex, Jablite and Rockwool, which are variously polyurethane, expanded polystyrene and mineral wool. They all have good websites and loads of marketing that tell you all you need to know about the products. They are mass produced, relatively cheap and easily available throughout the country. All are rated A or B on the Green Guide to Housing Specification (although that may change in the new Guide, due late 2007).

These are all highly processed materials carrying a high overhead in terms of energy consumed in production, and the consequent CO_2 emissions. It has to be said that the manufacturers are taking steps to reduce their carbon footprint, by recycling energy and installing renewable energy systems. Which helps, but also points at the high levels of energy they are using. They also trumpet their sustainable credentials by pointing at up to 50 percent material content being recycled. But the *other* 50 percent, as a minimum, is virgin material. They also claim that the insulation can itself be recycled, but in practice have these products

2

ever come out of a building to be reused?

When these products are installed they are generally cut to fit between joist or rafters, resulting in a fair quantity of offcuts. Most often those offcuts are popped into a skip and sent to landfill where, because they are non biodegradable, they will sit for eons.

Non-sustainable insulation products do the job they are intended to do, are cheap and readily available. But can they really form part of a sustainable build when there are so many options available?

MULTI-FOIL INSULATION

The most common of the multi-foils are Tri-Iso Super 9 or 10 and Thinsulex. They have a nominal thickness of 25mm to 30mm and are made up of 14 or 19 separate layers, the second set layers being a reversed repeat of the first set. The separate layers are then stitched or bonded together to form a quilt-like sheet.

There is some controversy over the thermal performance of this product. The manufacturer of Tri-Iso commissioned a report from TRADA Technology Ltd, which states " *"…TRI-ISO SUPER 9 had insulating properties equivalent to mineral wool (glass) of 200 mm. This provides thermal performance to the equivalent of an overall thermal resistance (RT) of 5 m^2K/W based on a recognised international thermal conductivity value for standard glass wool insulation of 0.04 W/m·K."*

This is a comparative test contrasting two insulation systems that does not provide any actual U-values or R-values. One or other of which is essential for BBA or EOTA approval (effectively the British or European kite marks).

In 2004 Celotex Ltd commissioned the National Physical Laboratories, Teddington, to undertake a hot-box test (the standard test for all UK insulation materials), which gave a measured thermal resistance of 1.71 m^2K/W, about one third of that indicated by TRADA. This equates to a U-value of 0.58, which is not too good but close to what would be expected from a material 30mm thick.

The Multifoil Manufacturers Association have always maintained that, uniquely, multi-foils perform better in-situ than in the hot-box test. To address this, in July 2005 the Building Research Establishment carried out in-situ measurement of the U-value of the product where Tri-Iso Super 9 was the principal or only insulation in walls, floor and roof constructions. The insulation was carried out to a number of similar houses on an estate in Scotland and the report provided to the ODPM runs to 12 pages but concludes

2

that the National Physical Laboratories are right.

The result of all this is that Local Authority Building Control has withdrawn approval for multi-foils as the principal or only insulation material, although some authorities still permit its use in loft conversions where there is insufficient space for standard insulation materials.

As with most things, there remains a role of multi-foil in tight situations, to help avoid cold-bridges and to improve air-tightness. If multi-foil remains the preferred option then the builder may be advised to look to Thinsulex from Web Dymanics. This is a very similar product to Tri-Iso but has BBA certification based on more sustainable claims and they provide better guidance on how best to use the product.

SUSTAINABLE INSULATION MATERIALS

SHEEP WOOL

The product's trade name is Thermafleece and it is produced by Second Nature UK, based in the Northern Lake District, from British hill sheep.

Sheep wool can be used in roofs and timber frame walls. In these areas it is best used with a permeable breather membrane on the cold side of the insulation. It can also be used in flooring, both in suspended timber ground floors and in intermediate timber floors. Again, a breather membrane is required.

As it is hygroscopic it helps to prevent condensation – wool absorbs 40 percent of its dry weight in moisture. Because wool generates heat when it absorbs moisture, it produces 960kj of heat energy for every kg of dry wool. This warmth isn't noticeable inside the building but acts to prevent condensation in cavities by maintaining the temperature.

Sheep wool uses just 14 percent of the energy used to produce glass fibre insulation so pays back manufacturing energy cost seven times faster. The only additives to the wool are Borax to prevent insect and fungal attack and a small quantity of viscose (recycled) to aid binding. This also means that it is fully

THERMAFLEECE

Thickness of Batt	Coverage per pack	Price per pack	Price per m^2
50mm	20.16m^2	£112.75	£5.60
75mm	12.96m^2	£108.43	£8.37
100mm	10.08m^2	£112.52	£11.16

The product is available from many sources, including www.greenbuildingstore.co.uk and www. naturalinsulations.co.uk

SIMPLY SUSTAINABLE HOMES

recyclable once it is removed.

It adapts to the shape of the cavity that it fills but also has a tendency to slump when used in walls, so needs to be held in place properly. When properly installed, it will have a life expectancy similar to that of the building. Its thermal and sound-insulation qualities are very similar to mineral wool and is in effect a direct replacement.

The www.secondnatureuk.com website contains a list of suppliers throughout the UK.

Thermafleece is the clear market leader and is sold in batts that are 1200mm long and either 400mm or 600mm wide. It is available in three thicknesses: 50mm, 75mm and 100mm.

FLAX

This is made from natural flax fibres that are held together with natural binders. The two leading trade names are Isovlas Flax and Flax 100. It is more difficult to find than sheep wool but it is available through www.ecomerchant.co.uk and www.greenandeasy.co.uk or www.constructionresources.com.

ISOVLAS

Batt Size	Coverage per pack	Price per pack	Price per m²
50mm x 600mm	7.2m²	£27.15	£3.77
100mm x 600mm	3.6m²	£30.89	£8.58
50mm x 400mm	4.8m²	£20.60	£4.29
100mm x 400mm	2.4m²	£18.09	£7.54

Isovlas is sold in packs of 10 batts. Each batt is 1200mm long and either 400mm or 600mm wide.

FLAX 100

Thickness of Batt	Coverage per pack	Price per m²
40mm	6.25m²	£5.50
50mm	5m²	£6.50
60mm	4.38m²	£8.00
80mm	3.12m²	£10.50
100mm	2.5m²	£13.33
120mm	1.88m²	£16.00
140mm	1.88m²	£18.50
160mm	1.88m²	£21.00
180mm	1.88m²	£23.50
200mm	1.25m²	£26.00

Flax 100 is sold in batts 1000mm long and 625mm wide. It is sold in a variety of thicknesses between 40mm and 200mm.

The properties of flax are very similar to sheep wool and it is suitable for the same applications. The major difference is that the flax fibres are bound with potato starch and so the product is entirely natural.

Like sheep wool, it is non toxic and non irritant so no specialist equipment is required for installation, which only requires a sharp knife and a keen eye.

CLOTH

Metisse Cloth Insulation

This is the product of a French social investment company, Le Relais, and has the trade name Metisse Cloth Insulation. The principal activity of the company is to provide employment opportunities within France and Africa. The employees collect old clothing and the good quality items are sent to Africa to remain as clothing, while what is left is turned into insulation.

The insulation is made from 80 percent recycled wool, cotton and acrylic. The remaining 20 percent is polyester added as a binder. Once again, it has very similar qualities to sheep wool and flax and is suitable for the same applications. Metisse comes in batt form.

Innotherm

Closer to home, Innotherm is another cloth insulation made from 100 percent recycled industrial cotton waste, which can be purchased directly from Recovery Insulation in Sheffield. As with most of these companies, they will deliver. Their product comes in batt and in roll form, but otherwise it is very like Metisse in its properties.

METISSE CLOTH

Batt Size	Coverage per pack	Price per pack	Price per m²
50mm x 600mm	21.6m²	£115.13	£5.33
100mm x 600mm	10,8m²	£80.24	£7.43
180mm x 600mm	5.76m²	£74.65	£12.96

This product only appears to be available from www.ecomerchant.co.uk

INNOTHERM

Batt/Roll size	Price per m²
75mm x 400mm	£6.40
100mm x 400mm	£8.50
100mm x 600mm	£8.50

All batts and rolls come in 1200mm lengths.

2

HEMP BATTS

Batt Size	Pack size (batts per pack)	Coverage per pack	Price per pack	Price per m²
50x385x1200mm	12	5.5m²	£25.40	£4.62
50x575x1200mm	12	8.3m²	£37.95	£4.57
75x385x1200mm	8	3.7m²	£24.45	£6.61
75x575x1200mm	8	5.5m²	£36.50	£6.66
100x385x1200mm	6	2.77m²	£23.40	£8.45
100x575x1200mm	6	4.14m²	£34.90	£8.43

Hemp

The trade name is ThermoHemp and it was the 2006 Grand Designs winner for 'Best Eco Product'. It is available primarily through an Irish company, Ecological Building Systems.

Since 1996, the cultivation of low narcotic hemp has been allowed in the UK. As it grows, hemp restricts environmental pollution because it absorbs CO_2, which is locked in to the material until it eventually decays. No herbicides or pesticides are needed during cultivation because it naturally repels pests and weeds. It has all the same advantages of sheep wool, flax and cotton but also has two properties that set it apart.

The first is that, being stiffer than other fibres, it is not prone to slump. This means that it does not form around pipes as well but also it will not drop in a wall to leave an insulation gap at the top. The second? It smells nice.

Thermo Hemp comes in roll and batt form with various sizes available. The batts are available in either 580mm or 375mm widths at 1200mm lengths and thicknesses of 30mm to 180mm. The rolls are available in lengths of 6m or 8m and 375mm or 580mm widths, with thicknesses of 30mm to 80mm.

The prices above apply to NBT Hemp Batts, produced by Natural Building Technologies, based in Buckinghamshire.

These hemp batts are slightly different in that the fibres are bound with a thermoplastic and are treated with inorganic salts to provide fire and pest resistance. This particular form of hemp insulation should not be used in cavity walls or under ground floors. In all other respects, it is the same as Thermo Hemp and sells through a number of national and well-known suppliers, including Travis Perkins and Jewson.

ISONAT

Thickness	Width	Number of batts per pack	Coverage per pack	Price per pack	Price per m²
50mm	400mm	12	5.76m²	£22.75	£3.95
50mm	600mm	12	8.64m²	£34.12	£3.95
75mm	400mm	8	3.84m²	£22.85	£5.95
75mm	600mm	8	5.76m²	£34.27	£5.95
100mm	400mm	8	2.88m²	£22.75	£7.90
100mm	600mm	8	4.32m²	£34.08	£7.90

The product is available from Sustainable Building Supplies and Natural Insulations.

ISONAT

Isonat is made from UK grown hemp and cotton waste although the final product is manufactured in France. It also contains 15 percent polyester fibres as a binder. As with NBT Hemp it is treated with inorganic salts, and prolonged exposure to water will cause it to decay.

Isonat is produced in batts all measuring 1200mm in length.

WOOD FIBRE

This is a huge area with a large number of different products, although there are only three main manufacturers.

HOMATHERM

Homatherm WoodFlex Protect

A medium-density semi-rigid insulation in batt form. It is made from wood chippings with 7-10 percent polyolefin fibres. It is suitable for all timber frame constructions – walls, floors and roofs. Cellulose fibres enable absorption of 17 percent moisture without losing thermal performance. This protects the building structure since the moisture is absorbed by the insulation rather than the structural timbers. The polyolefin fibres are added to provide a degree of flexibility in all directions.

2

HOMATHERM WOODFLEX PROTECT

Thickness	Length and width (mm)	Coverage per pack	Price per pack	Price per m²
60mm	1250 x 570	3.6m²	£41.75	£11.72
80mm	1200 x 625	3m²	£42.75	£14.25
80mm	1250 x 570	2.85m²	£40.65	£14.26
100mm	1200 x 625	2.25m²	£40.08	£17.81
100mm	1250 x 570	2.14m²	£37.14	£17.38
120mm	1200 x 625	2.25m²	£45.86	£20.38
140mm	1200 x 625	1.5m²	£34.50	£23.00
140mm	1200 x 570	1.37m²	£31.50	£23.03
180mm	1200 x 625	1.5m²	£44.32	£29.55
200mm	1200 x 625	1.5m²	£48.65	£32.43
200mm	1250 x 570	1.425m²	£46.22	£32.44

The product is available from Construction Resources and Ecological Building Systems.

THERMOWALL 040 & 045

Thickness	Length and Width	Coverage per pack	Price per pack	Price per m²
Standard size				
40mm	1190 x 590	70.21m²	£786.35	£11.20
60mm	1190 x 590	46.34m²	£967.58	£20.88
Large Size				
40mm	1250 x 2600	81.25m²	£1090.00	£38.81
60mm	1250 x 2600	52m²	£1055.00	£37.57

As with Homatherm, the main supplier of Thermowall is Construction Resources.

GUTEX

2

Thermowall 040 and 045

Gutex is a German company and all of their products are manufactured from the by-products of the sawmills of southern Germany. The softwood chippings are pulped and soaked in water before they are mechanically pressed into boards, dried and cut to shape. In the case of Thermowall, boards that are thicker than 20mm are made up of 20mm thick laminations. Durability is said to be 70 years+ (which sounds a long time, but is probably less than the life of the building), the product has no chemical additives, no toxins or toxic emissions and is CO_2 zero rated.

It is particularly useful as external cladding on timber frame as it is able to accept cement or lime render.

It also displays slightly better thermal resistance than low-density fibres (wool, flax, cotton, etc) although it is a good deal more expensive. It is one to use for particular applications.

ThermoSafe 040

This is a rigid insulation board manufactured in exactly the same way as Thermowall and is suitable for flooring (below the screed), walls (internal and external) and roofs. It comprises 97 percent wood chippings, 2 percent water and 1 percent natural resin adhesive. All other properties are exactly the same as Thermowall.

Boards are available in the dimensions displayed in the chart bottom right.

UltraTherm 045

Another rigid insulation, although this comes in a tongue and groove format ideally suited for the thermal upgrading of existing roof constructions. In effect, it is a high-performance sarking board that is also suitable for externally insulating timber frames or green oak-framed buildings. Due to a factory applied coating it is also suitable for use as a temporary wall/roof covering. These qualities mean that it can also be used to eliminate cold bridging through

THERMOSAFE 040

Board Size	Thickness	Price per pallet	Coverage per pallet
1200mm x 600mm	40mm	100	72m²
1200mm x 600mm	60mm	66	47.5m²
1200mm x 600mm	100mm	40	28.8m²

This product available from Construction Resources.

2

ULTRATHERM 045

Thickness	Coverage per board	Boards per pallet	Coverage per pack	Cost per pallet	Price per m²
All boards measure 1780mm in length and 600mm width					
50mm	0.84m²	40	42.72m2	£753	£17.63
60mm	0.84m²	34	36.31m2	£730	£20.51
100mm	0.84m²	20	21.36m2	£659	£30.28
120mm	0.84m²	18	19.22m2	£700	£36.42

This product available from Construction Resources.

timbers and can act as an insulating sheathing board for timber frames.

PAVATEX

Pavatex is exactly the same as all of the above in that it is produced from waste wood materials and is 100 percent natural. All Pavatex boards are supplied with fully compatible fixings, renders and accessories. The boards are manufactured in Switzerland and consist of 99.5 percent waste softwood and 0.5 percent inert waterproofing. It can be used for new buildings, applied directly to timber or steel frames, and to all types of masonry. It can also be used for external and internal insulation and in renovations.

These products have an interlock system on all four sides, which can provide complete wind and water tightness. It comes in boards measuring 2500mm in length and 770mm in width. There are three thicknesses available – 22mm, 35mm and 60mm.

Pavatherm Plus

Pavatherm is made from 99.5 percent waste softwood and 0.5 percent paraffin. When the boards are produced the wood fibres are pulped and mixed with water. The pulp is then heated to activate the natural lignin in order to glue the fibres together and the pulp is then mechanically pressed into boards. Pavatherm Plus can be used like Isolair on walls, but not on roofs. Isolair is roof specific

and Pavatherm Plus is wall specific.

The boards are tongue and groove so that they interlock on all four sides and this material is typically used directly underneath external timber cladding. Being hygroscopic means that a vapour permeable membrane is unnecessary. The product itself keeps the building structure dry. Being air tight and rigid means that the insulation performance can be guaranteed for the life of the building.

In timber frames it is suggested that Pavatherm be used with another form of insulation such as Warmcel or hemp. On masonry constructions, the Pavatherm boards can be attached directly to the masonry substrate but the product can only be installed by competent contractors.

The main UK supplier used by Pavatex is New Building Technologies and they in turn sell through the suppliers listed previously for the hemp batts.

DIFFUTHERM

This is an external wall insulation that can be used on timber frames and masonry walls as with all the Pavatex products. It is available through Calch Ty-Mawr Lime (www.lime.org.uk). As with all the others though, it can be purchased through NBT and Sustainable Building Supplies.

It should be, and can be, sold together with a Bayosan thin-mesh coat render. In timber frames it can be used as an external insulation in conjunction with a 'vapour open' insulation like sheep wool or cotton and again can only be installed by approved contractors who have

DIFFUTHERM

Thickness	Length and width	Number of boards	Coverage per pack	Price per m²	Price per board
20 mm	60mm x 120mm	8	5.8m²	£6.07	£4.40
40 mm	60mm x120mm	4	2.92m²	£12.26	£8.95
60 mm	1300mm x 790mm	30	30.19m²	£19.77	£19.90
80 mm	1300mm x 790mm	22	22.14m²	£26.43	£26.60
100 mm	1300mm x 790mm	18	8.11m²	£32.99	£33.20

This product is available through Calch Ty-Mawr Lime (www.lime.org.uk)

2

been trained by NBT.

Diffutherm can also be used as an internal insulation for walls, floors and ceilings and for upgrading the insulation in existing buildings, both solid walls and brick-infilled traditional timber frames.

RECYCLED PAPER OR CELLULOSE

Trade names for this material are Warmcel, Vital 040 and Termex. Its stands alongside sheep wool in terms of its impact on the market.

Warmcel

Produced by a company called Excel Building Solutions, based in Gwent, who supply across Europe. It is made from 100 percent recycled paper and is available in a number of forms – Warmcel 100, Warmcel 500, Warmcel 300, Warmcel RF.

Warmcel 100

This is specifically used for DIY loft insulation and can simply be emptied from the bag into the loft space, and spread by hand. It is non toxic and non irritant and uses inorganic salts to increase fire resistance. It is resistant to biological and fungal attack and unattractive to vermin.

Thermal conductivity of 0.036 W/m.K is the same as sheep wool, flax, hemp and cotton, but performance is enhanced by its ability to create a high level of air tightness to prevent thermal convection currents if the insulation is firmly compacted.

One Bag Covers
100mm = 2.5m², 150mm = 1.6m², 200mm = 1.2m², 250mm =1m²

Warmcel 500

This is used for EVT Technology applications, specifically EVT walls, roofs and floors. An EVT construction (used as a structural wall or roof) combines high levels of insulation with the ability to control the migration of any moisture that gets into the structure (which happens in any inhabited building) to the external side of the structure where it is harmlessly expelled to the atmosphere. This action, known as 'Enhance Vapour Transfer' or EVT, ensures that interstitial condensation does not occur, thereby protecting the

2

timber structure throughout the lifetime of the building. The product is usually turbo-filled or damp spray installed.

The significance of this is that a major company in the home building industry, Excel Industries Ltd, is specifically using a natural insulation material because of the properties that it brings. As well as having the lowest embodied energy of sustainable insulation materials, in this case they are using its hygroscopic qualities to provide a natural means of controlling and directing condensation.

Warmcel 300

As Warmcell 500, but specifically for new build lofts, floors or other open horizontal surfaces. It is dry blown to fill between and over joists.

Warmcel RF

Designed for retrofit installation into older properties for lofts and cavity walls. It is dry blown by specialists and can be used if there is no insulation at all or as a top up over existing insulation.

Turbo filling – a method used for closed panel structures. A hole is drilled into the wall, a hose is attached and the Warmcel is sprayed into the cavity.

Damp Spraying – use for open panels. The Warmcel is dampened, sprayed onto the wall and then levelled off to the depth of the studs. The moisture dries out naturally.

Warmcel is readily available with suppliers across the country through Pen Y Coed Construction (www.penycoed-warmcel. com) in Powys, Ecomerchant, the Low Impact Living Initiative (lowimpact.org.uk) and the South Yorkshire Energy Centre (syec.co.uk).

Ecomerchant are the cheapest at £6.75 per 8kg bag.

Vital 040

A cellulose insulation batt made from oxygen bleached wood pulp and viscose fibres. It also contains a food grade

VITAL 040

Batt Thickness	Coverage per pack	Price per pack	Price per m^2
Batts are 870mm by 565mm wide			
50mm	5.90m^2	£36.88	£6.25
100mm	2.95m^2	£36.88	£12.50
150mm	1.97m^2	£38.22	£19.40

This product available from Construction Resources

2

cellulose-based binder and a ph neutral boron liquid to provide permanent protection against fire and mould. It can absorb 20 percent moisture without losing any significant thermal performance – seven times more than a mineral wool product of similar density. It is a semi-rigid product, manufactured in Finland.

Termex

Another product from recycled newsprint produced in Finland from paper where vegetable-oil based pigments are used for the ink. In all other respects the same as Warmcell and Vital but with a very slightly better thermal performance.

TERMEX

Depth of Termex	U Value	Price per m2
100mm	0.400	£5.19
150mm	0.267	£7.79
200mm	0.200	£10.37
250mm	0.160	£12.99
300mm	0.133	£15.57
350mm	0.114	£18.14
400mm	0.100	£20.75

Available from Termex UK Ltd in York.

Homatherm flexCL

This product is from recycled newspaper, with added jute sacking. It comes in batt form with a slightly higher density than other cellulose products giving a better acoustic performance.

HOMATHERM FLEXCL

Batt Thickness	Coverage per pack	Price per m^2	Price per pack	Coverage per pallet	Price per m^2	Price per pallet	Packs per pallet
Batts come in lengths of 1200mm and widths of 625mm							
30mm	7.5m^2	£6.40	£48.00	105m^2	£5.61	£589.23	14
40mm	6.0m^2	£6.59	£39.56	84.0m^2	£6.15	£516.89	14
50mm	4.5m^2	£10.62	£47.81	63m^2	£9.94	£626.06	14
60mm	3.75m^2	£12.07	£45.28	52.5m^2	£11.29	£592.72	14
80mm	3m^2	£14.25	£42.75	42m^2	£13.31	£559.13	14
100mm	2.25m^2	£17.81	£40.08	31.5m^2	£16.63	£523.69	14
120mm	2.25m^2	£20.38	£45.86	27m^2	£19.06	£514.62	12
140mm	1.5m^2	£23.00	£34.50	24m^2	£21.50	£516.00	12
160mm	1.5m^2	£26.25	£39.38	21m^2	£24.50	£514.50	12
180mm	1.5m^2	£29.55	£44.32	18m^2	£27.26	£490.70	12

This product available from Construction Resources.

CORKBOARD

2

Cork works as an insulation material because slightly over 50 percent of the volume is air trapped within the cell structure. It is normally supplied in board form, which is manufactured from cork granules that are re-formed under heat and pressure and bonded together using natural cork resins. It displays very similar properties to wood fibre boards in terms of thermal performance, acoustics, fire resistance and processing energy. Cork is available in thinner sections than wood fibre boards, down to just 12mm, which makes it useful in renovations as floor and wall insulation.

The cork oak is a forest tree that grows in Spain, Portugal and North Africa. Cork bark is harvested from trees 20 to 30 years old with an optimum harvesting cycle of every nine to 12 years. There is some concern that the stock of this slow-growing tree is not able to meet the demands of the modern world. The temptation is to shorten the harvesting cycle, giving a higher annual output but damaging, and potentially killing, the tree.

Cork flooring and insulation is available from many sources, one of which is www.westcofloors.co.uk

WHAT YOU DON'T GET FROM SUSTAINABLE INSULATION

Sustainable insulation will cost more. In terms of a whole house it could be 50 percent to 100 percent more. It is not produced in the same volumes as non-sustainable materials and has some way to go before those economies of scale kick in. Considered as a proportion of the overall project cost this uplift is relatively small and what you don't get from sustainable insulation is:

Itchy hands, Sore eyes, Gassing off, a Health & Safety leaflet

DRAUGHT PROOFING

Less of a problem with new build than renovation or refurbishment. The DTI suggest that 10 percent of the heat lost from a house is via draughts although it is not clear if this figure attributes to old, draughty houses or more modern properties.

It takes a person with dedication, persistence and without the burden of a full-time job to achieve a 100 percent draught-free house. And, in truth, some air movement is necessary if for no other reason than to keep the oxygen refreshed. It is the unknown, uncontrollable

2

draughts under doors, around windows, from disused flues that are the problem. The most overlooked draughts in older properties are those from the joint of the ground floor and the wall, especially where there is a suspended floor.

Sealing the obvious gaps is a fairly simple and cheap operation. There are many products available in the local DIY shed, from brush strips to mastics. It has been estimated that draught-proofing a three-bedroom Victorian house will cost £50 to £100.

RADIATOR REFLECTORS

It is obvious when you think about it that a proportion of the heat from a radiator is absorbed by the wall behind it. Which is not a wholly bad thing if the wall itself is well insulated as some of that heat will be leached back into the room when the radiator is turned off.

Once again, your local DIY shed is likely to stock a sticky-back tin foil sheet, designed specifically for the purpose. It is tricky to fit as it entails moving the radiator from the wall but the DTI tell us that it will save another 5 percent to 10 percent heat loss.

INSULATING THE VICTORIAN TERRACED HOUSE

How to approach insulation in a renovation project will depend to a large extent on the scope of the renovation. Lifting floorboards may not be part of the plan if the renovation is more geared towards a quick lick of paint. But there are still things to do.

Roof

30 percent of the heat lost from the building will be through the roof, and lofts generally benefit from a bit of extra insulation. Any of the hemp, cotton, wool or cellulose materials are great in the loft and extremely easy to work with, especially if the loft necessitates crawling about on hands and knees.

A minimum of 270mm should be installed but this should be increased if there is little opportunity to properly insulate walls and floor; 300mm or even 350mm is not out of the question. The point at which the energy used in the manufacturer of the insulation is outweighed by the energy saved by the insulation is 1m thick.

Walls

35 percent of the heat lost from the building is through the walls and Victorian walls tend to be 9in of solid brick. Older houses

2

with cavity walls are easy to deal with by getting in a cavity wall insulation specialist. It will cost a few pounds, depending on the size of the house and will have a dramatic impact on the warmth of the property and the fuel bill. Whether sustainable materials can be used will depend on the situation but it is well worth asking, particularly for Warmcell.

Solid walls are usually only insulated with an interior cladding. Of the sustainable materials the wood fibres and cork are the best options. Pavatherm and Thermosafe are both suitable for walls and can be plastered or wall-papered over.

If there is insufficient room for a wood fibre board Sempatap wall lining may be an answer. It is a latex based product that can be glued to the wall and improves the thermal performance of the wall by about 20 percent. It is just 5mm thick and therefore has little impact where it meets door or window frames. But a note of caution. Sempatap does not meet fire regulations for buildings with public access (holiday homes, B&B would fall into this category).

Ground Floor

Another 20 percent to 25 percent of the heat will be lost through the ground floor. For a suspended timber floor there is no better option than taking up the floor-boards and installing a quilt or board insulation. Almost all of the sustainable materials will work well. At least 100mm quilt will be needed, 200mm would not be out of place if space allows.

For a solid floor or where boards cannot be raised insulate on top with a wood fibre board or cork or, if thickness is an issue, Sempafloor.

Windows and Doors

In renovating older properties, style and appearance will be important factors. Replacing existing wooden windows with uPVC double glazing will cost a lot of money and could be a stylistic disaster. The ubiquitous uPVC or PVCu frames that we see everywhere are an environmental nightmare (especially the wood-effect ones which even look like a nightmare). They use a huge amount of energy to produce and the production process releases high levels of dioxins and other carcinogenic chemicals. And they are non recyclable when you are finished with them.

On the other hand, Victorian sliding sashes are draughty and have a ridiculously high U-value, usually over 5 (compared to 1.8 for modern double glazing). Having said that, the payback period on replacement double glazing is around 94 years.

A 9in solid brick wall will have a U-value of 2.2 $W/m^2/^{0}C$. With some internal insulation that will come down to perhaps 1.8 – the same as a modern double-glazed window. So it is

2

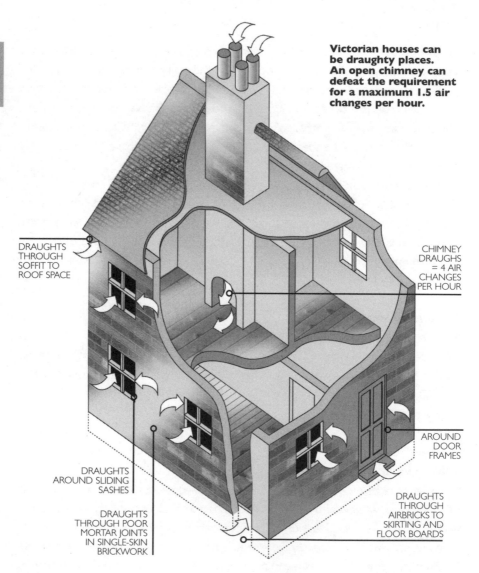

Victorian houses can be draughty places. An open chimney can defeat the requirement for a maximum 1.5 air changes per hour.

DRAUGHTS THROUGH SOFFIT TO ROOF SPACE

CHIMNEY DRAUGHS = 4 AIR CHANGES PER HOUR

DRAUGHTS AROUND SLIDING SASHES

DRAUGHTS THROUGH POOR MORTAR JOINTS IN SINGLE-SKIN BRICKWORK

AROUND DOOR FRAMES

DRAUGHTS THROUGH AIRBRICKS TO SKIRTING AND FLOOR BOARDS

important to do something about those Victorian sliding sashes.

There are two possible answers. Retain the frames if they are in reasonable condition, draught proof the sashes with brush strips and replace the glazing with double glazed units. The units will have a narrower gap than is usual, possibly 6mm or 8mm, but will still improve thermal performance.

Alternatively, secondary double glazing may be the answer. There are lots of options available, from polythene film

(from your local DIY store) held in place with double-sided tape and blown with a hair dryer to get the wrinkles out, to metal framed glass, held in place with magnets for easy cleaning. Both will eliminate drafts and significantly improve the U-value.

A similar argument holds for doors. A solid timber door, typical in older properties, has a U-value of 2.4, compared to 2.2 for a uPVC door. Eliminating the draughts around the door will achieve a comparable U-value and retain the good looks of the original door.

Chimneys

If a fireplace is to be retained and used, there is no way of stopping the draughts when the fire is not lit. If the fireplace is not to be used, then blocking the flue with masonry will effectively block the draughts. But be aware that chimneys and chimney stacks tend to let in rain water and the flue is a natural means of keeping the chimney, and surrounding walls, dry. If the flue is blocked at the fireplace end then care has to be taken to ensure no water gets in at the stack end.

Air bricks

Air bricks are installed for one of two reasons; to vent a room with an open fire or boiler to make sure there is enough air to support the combustion, or to vent timber floors and cavities to prevent damp and rot. In either case the air brick is likely to cause draughts but those draughts are necessary if the air brick still has a function to fulfil.

IN SUMMARY

Improving air tightness and eliminating draughts is a requirement under current Building Regulations. Whether it is a good idea is open to question, but it remains a statutory requirement nonetheless. Installing high levels of insulation is also a statutory requirement and makes good practical and commercial sense. Using sustainable insulation materials offers no benefit in terms of thermal performance, but the benefits in terms of their impact on the environment, the house and the people that live in it are many.

3 RENEWABLE ENERGY THE FACTS

B arely a day goes by without a Government policy announcement on sustainability. Proposals for compulsory carbon emission targets in the Climate Change Bill could have a significant impact on the way we design and run houses.

Renewable-energy technologies are generally referred to by the Government as Low and Zero Carbon (LZC) technologies and the attention they receive is mostly focused on a few high-profile schemes – large wind farms and Mr David Cameron's little turbine. However, since all buildings must eventually reduce their carbon emissions small-scale renewables need to provide an effective solution.

The UK housing stock uses 27 percent of the nation's energy and it therefore presents a number of challenges. A high-proportion of the stock is old, poorly-insulated homes that have low-efficiency heating and lighting. In addition, consumption of energy in the home is increasing, as greater personal wealth results in a growing list of appliances and gadgets. Also the density of the UK's occupation of housing is falling (high divorce rate = more sole occupants), and small households produce disproportionately high carbon emissions.

The optimum strategy for cutting carbon emissions is reducing the need for energy in the first place. Changing occupant behaviour and improving the thermal performance of buildings are the most effective ways of reducing emissions, particularly as, in the case of building fabric, once an improvement is made, savings continue for the life of the building.

However, as carbon reductions of 60 percent are needed to meet long-term targets, LZC sources are important too. There are basically three kinds of LZC technology: that which provides heat, that which provides electricity and that which provides both.

There is also that which provides none of the above. That we call eco-bling. Eco-bling is stuff, typically a solar panel or a wind turbine, that is bolted to a house with no real hope that it will achieve anything. People do it for the same reason that they wear bling – because

COURTSEY PROVEN ENERGY

Proven 2.5kW

it looks good and they want to be seen to be green without putting too much effort into establishing just how green they really are. The point of renewable energy is that it puts control of energy production in the hands of the home owner and limits the CO_2 emissions from that house. Eco-bling does not give control and merely adds to the CO_2 problem.

ENERGY USE IN THE HOME

We use energy as either heat or power – heat for keeping us warm, for hot water and cooking and power to run TVs, DVDs, kettles, computers etc.

If we comply with current building regulations on insulation 53 percent of the energy we use will go in heating, 20 percent on hot water, 16 percent to power appliances, 6 percent on lighting and 5 percent on cooking (Figures from Energy Saving Trust – May 2007). Or 73 percent on heat and 27 percent on power. If your house was built before 2004 and has not had the insulation upgraded then the proportion is more likely to be 84 percent on heat and 16 percent on power.

Renewable energy, like everything else in the home, will have a budget around it. Very few of us can throw enough money at the problem to make it go away and if you are thinking about how best to use a limited budget, think about heat first, hot water second and power last.

3

PAY BACK

One of the major issues around renewable energy is still its financial viability.

Looked at as individual components the pay-back on any renewable technology tends to be high – in the region of 10 to 20 years or more. On the other hand, a well-designed system meeting a high proportion of the household needs should pay for itself in less than 10 years. Still a long time and too long for many.

But consider this. What is the pay-back on an Aga or Rayburn? Why do we choose to install a £15,000 William Ball kitchen rather than a £1,500 kitchen from IKEA? We make choices about what to put in our homes for reasons of aesthetics, comfort, style, because they add value to the property and because they make us feel good. Why do we then demand that renewable energy, and only renewable energy, gives us a return on our investment?

If you are building or renovating your home, not installing some renewable energy would seem to be missing a trick. It will never be as cheap or so easy to install as when you have other works going on. And it is likely to become mandatory in the not too distant future. Currently, under Planning Policy Statement 22, or Technical Advice Note 8 in Wales, all developments of 10 properties or more must generate at least 10 percent of the energy consumed on site, although these are guidelines rather than rules. Ruth Kelly has said that the Government's aim is that ALL new buildings will be carbon neutral by 2016. Carwyn Jones, the Welsh Assembly energy minister, has given Wales until 2012 to achieve the same thing.

Clarification from the two Governments confirms that they mean ALL buildings – which includes the individual home of the self builder. In addition, it is likely to be extended to encompass major renovations.

An incredible 27 percent of all the energy consumed in the UK is used in the home. There is little wonder then that the various Governments are pushing us to do it ourselves. It may help with CO_2 emissions and it may help combat global warming, but it will certainly mean that the Government has to invest in fewer power stations.

But perhaps more importantly for the individual, it gives us more control. We are an oil-based society and North Sea oil has been a boon to the whole of the UK. It has given us cheap fuel, relative to the rest of Europe, for 40 years and allowed us to become the fourth-richest nation in the world.

But natural gas from the North Sea has all but run out and the oil will follow soon. Oil is obviously a finite resource. The world is not making any more of it and the rate at which we can find and extract oil is, for the first time in history, being outstripped by the increase in demand. It now costs 1.8 barrels of oil (in equivalent energy terms) to produce one barrel of oil. And production can no longer keep up with the rate at which developing countries are consuming it. To put it another way, as demand increases and supply falls oil is only going to get more expensive.

Renewable energy allows us to step aside from the oil economy. Producing energy by other means provides us with security, insurance perhaps, against whatever will occur in the energy market.

Pay back will soon be a complete irrelevance. Not that long ago central heating increased the value of the property – it was considered an uncommon but desirable and saleable feature. Now not having central heating is odd and deflates the value of a house. In 2005, 85 percent of all new homes in Austria had wood pellet boilers fitted as standard (Austria does not have oil, but does have some trees). Wood, in the form of pellets, is now their de facto standard heating fuel. In Demark, street heating – where a whole street of houses is heated and powered by a single, central, often wood-pellet fuelled, combined heat and power system – is commonplace.

The UK will take its own spin on things, but it is difficult to believe that in 20 year's time, there will be no change in the way UK houses are heated. People who install renewable energy systems now will have that uncommon but desirable and saleable feature. They will sow the financial investment that their children will reap.

CALCULATING HEAT LOSS

Whether you're installing a heat pump or a gas boiler, you need to know how much heat you need to produce. Standard gas or oil-fired boilers have a wide modulation range – that is the amount of heat they produce at any moment can vary within a range, which could be as wide as 4kW to 24kW. Renewable energy technologies tend to impose tighter limits and it is important to be sure you are in the right range.

Below is a simple method of calculating the heat loss from your property. It does NOT replace a full SAP calculation but is quick, easy and relatively accurate.

The calculation is based on our standard house. Area is simply the measured area of the element in square metres, as is the volume. The U-Value is explained in Section 1 and the figures used here are considered best practice by the Energy Saving Trust.

The temperature difference is for a (increasingly less) common winter day; so an outside air temperature of -2°C with an inside temperature of 22°C in main areas will give a

3

HEAT LOSS CALCULATION WITH BEST PRACTICE INSULATION LEVELS

Element	Area	Volume	U-value	Temp difference	Heat loss	Corrected Heat loss
Doors: solid	1.8		3	24	129.60	198
Doors: glazed	5.4		2.2	24	285.12	436
Windows: single glazed	0		5	24	0.00	0
Windows: double glazed - Low E	22.5		1.8	24	972.00	1486
Roof Lights: double glazed Low E	1.5		1.8	24	64.80	99
Ground Floor: insulated	100		0.22	24	528.00	807
First Floor	100		0.18	22	396.00	605
Walls: cavity, net of windows	172		0.35	23	1384.60	2116
Roof	135		0.16	22	475.20	726
Ventilation	480	0.3		23	3312.00	5063

Total Heat Loss	**7547.32**
Total Corrected Heat Loss - Watts	**11537**
Casual Gains	**850**
Heating load	**Watts =10687**
	EQUATES TO 53.4 WATTS PER SQ M

temperature difference of 24⁰C.

Heat loss is a simple multiplication of area x U-value x temperature difference and the corrected heat loss applies a coefficient to allow for system inefficiencies.

The calculation assumes an ideal level of insulation and produces a heat load of 10.6kW. That means that your principal heat source must have a rated output of at least that amount to meet the space heating requirement.

If we assume that the heating will be on from 6:30am to 8:30am, while we have breakfast and get ready for work and school, and again from 4:30pm to 10:30pm then we have a total running time of eight hours per day. If we also assume a heating season of 220 days per year (effectively October to May) then we have (8 x 220) 1760 running hours per year. At 10.6kW this equals 18,656kWh per year.

3

In addition, the house will need hot water. Assuming four people in occupation and a normal hot water demand of 50 litres per person per day, the energy requirement is:

200 litres × 1.16 watts × 50°C = 11,600 watts. A three-hour reheat time means a heating load of 3.9kW.

The reheat time is the amount of time you are prepared to wait for a tank full of cold water (if everyone has had a bath and you have used all the hot water) to come back up to temperature. Two or three hours is generally considered acceptable.

If the boiler is running for eight hours per day to provide space heating then the output capacity need only increase by 1.45kW to meet the hot water needed.

So going through the annual consumption calculation above we need 12.05kW for eight hours per day for 220 days per year, which equals 21,208kWh per year, plus 3.9kW for three hours per day for the other 145 days of the year to meet the hot water demand, which equals 1,696kWh per year – a total consumption of 22,904kWhpa.

Below is a running comparison chart. The figures assume newish, condensing type boilers. Non-condensing and older boilers can have efficiency levels as low as 65 percent.

The price per kWh will vary with the supplier and it has to be borne in mind that the price of oil, gas (including LPG) and electricity have increased by between 80 percent and 100 percent in the past three years. Biomass in the form of wood chip has increased by about 10 percent and wood pellet has fallen in price.

Probably the only thing we can be sure of is that these figures are not accurate. Oil, and consequently gas and electricity, prices will not increase 20 percent every year for five years and wood pellet prices will not plateau. But they serve to illustrate the relative differences in

RUNNING COST COMPARISON

To produce that same amount of heat will cost :-

Fuel	Equipment	Efficiency	Price per KWh	Annual cost
Natural Gas	Condensing boiler	85%	4.5p	£1,215
LPG	Condensing boiler	85%	12p	£3,240
Oil	Condensing boiler	85%	3.8p	£1,026
Ground source heat pump	Horizontal array	COP 4	3.12p	£842
Water Source heat pump	From borehole	COP 5	2.5p	£675
Wood Pellet	Boiler	90%	4.8p	£1,296
Wood Chip	Boiler	80%	2.8p	£756

3

capital and running cost increase in the initial investment.

It should also be borne in mind that the oil-fired boiler will be nearing the end of its life at 10 years. Efficiency will start to fall, fuel consumption will increase as well as emissions. The heat pump and wood pellet boiler will have a life of at least 15 years without any noticeable reduction in efficiency.

HEATING DISTRIBUTION

Before plumping for a particular heat source, decide on your distribution system. Basically this comes down to radiators or underfloor heating. There are other options like hot skirting boards, forced air and even hot ceilings, but these have a very small proportion of the market and that proportion has not grown significantly so we focus only on the two main options.

The issue is the optimum temperature at which the delivery system will operate. As will be seen, different heat sources also operate best at different temperatures and matching the two – heat source and distribution system – is essential to an efficient system.

5 YEAR FUEL COSTS

Year	Oil-Fired boiler	Ground source heat pump	Wood pellet boiler
Capital cost (1)			
	2,700	8,000	11,000
Year 1 running cost			
	1,026	842	1,296
Year 2 (2)	1,231	1,010	1,361
Year 3	1,477	1,212	1,429
Year 4	1,773	1,455	1,500
Year 5	2,127	1,746	1,575
5 Year running cost			
	10,377	14,265	18,161

(1) Average installed cost, assuming good quality equipment of comparable output. To include fuel storage facility as necessary.

(2) Assume that oil and electricity prices rise by 20% p.a. and that wood pellets rise at 5% (in line with historic rises).

(3) Includes running cost and capital cost of purchase and installation.

Optimum operating temperatures for the main methods are:

Underfloor heating	30-45°C
Low temperature radiators	45-55°C
Conventional radiators	60-80°C

3

There are other factors that will affect the choice of heating distribution system, like comfort, aesthetics, available wall space and these are all a matter of personal choice. In sustainability terms because underfloor heating operates at a lower temperature it uses less energy. If you want sustainable credentials you have to have a good reason to use anything else.

RENEWABLE TECHNOLOGIES

I. COMBINED HEAT AND POWER

Often referred to as micro-CHP, it is essentially an engine that powers a small generator. It is called combined heat and power because it produces both heat and electricity. In this way it is a very efficient use of the fuel consumed.

Micro-CHP, ie domestic scale, is still a rarity in the UK and CHP tends to be associated with large installations, such as in hospitals, leisure centres and the like. As at the end of 2005, about 1,500 CHP engines were in operation in the UK, only a few hundred of which are domestic scale.

Set against that are the assertions of the industry and the DTI that some 12 million homes in the UK are suitable candidates for micro-CHP. Which perhaps answers why the technology is moving to the forefront.

In its simplest form, a CHP plant is a standard internal combustion engine driving a largish alternator – just like you would have in your car. The heat from the engine is captured (sometimes exhaust heat is also captured) and the alternator will produce 240v or 440v electricity rather than 12v.

Powergen are soon to introduce the Whispergen machine which uses a Stirling engine. The Stirling engine is an *external* combustion engine, invented in the 19th century by Rev Robert Stirling. It is used a good deal in CHP as it is particularly good at producing a steady output with low

Whispergen from Powergen is one of only a handful of CHP available for domestic use.

3

noise. At the domestic scale the attraction of this engine is its higher energy conversion efficiency and its lower noise levels.

CHP units will run on gas (natural or LPG), oil (diesel or kerosene) or wood. Wood pellet or wood chip fuel machines tend to be large – 100KW plus – although there are a couple of domestic scale machines emerging. Most notable is the Sunmachine unit from Switzerland which runs on wood pellet. But at £15,000 it is likely to be some time before it makes an impact on the UK housing market.

There is currently a good deal of research in fuel cell technology, using gas (hydrogen, methane, natual gas of LPG) passing through a fuel cell to generate electricity. This technology is also being explored for the automotive industry but so far has not produced a usable product. At a domestic scale there is currently only a choice between the Whispergen from Powergen or the Senertec-Dachs from Baxi. These machines run on natural gas, LPG or kerosene and as such are not renewable energy – still reliant on the oil market and fluctuating utility prices. In housholds that have natural gas available the high levels of efficiency and relatively low carbon emissions make them an attractive proposition. Both operate at relatively high temperatures – 70°C to 80°C – and can be used with either radiators or underfloor heating.

Buying that same amount of electricity and gas from the grid would cost £1,410 for the Whispergen and over £2,500 for the Senertec. The cost per kWh shows that the output and efficiency is about the same but the ratio of heat to electricity is 8:1 for the Whispergen and 2.3:1 for the Senertec. The reason for that is that the Senertec uses a conventional single-cylinder internal combustion engine, which produces a good deal more heat for the power output.

The cost per kWh also shows that the cost of the heat alone is little more than the price of the gas used to produce it. The

FUEL CELL TECHNOLOGY

Supplier	Whispergen E.ON Powergen	Senertec-Dachs Baxi
Capital cost	£3,000	£12,000
Rated electrical output	1KW	5.5KW
Rated thermal output	8KW	12.5KW
Running time (per day)	11 hours[1]	7 hours
Thermal output (p.a.)	32,000[2]	32,000
Electrical output (p.a.)	4,000[3]	14,052
Running cost (p.a.)	£1,130[4]	£1,456
Cost per Kwh	3.14p	3.16p

(1) The time required to generate sufficient heat and hot water for the home
(2) Assume a heating demand spread over 365 days per year (rather than a 220 day heating season)
(3) Represents the target household electrical consumption
(4) Assumes a natural gas price of 3p per KWh – which will vary with supplier.

electricity produced is significantly lower than the grid price. The reason for this lies in efficiency. Electricity coming out of the 13amp socket represents less than 30 percent of the energy that went into the power station. Both the Senertec and the Whispergen are working on efficiencies of 95 percent. This efficiency is also reflected in carbon emissions which will be 1.5 to 2.9 tonnes per annum less with CHP than conventional generation.

Of course, the Senertec produces a good deal more electricity than the household can use, and the surplus can be sold to the grid. Prices are not great at the moment – 3.6p to 5p per kWh – but legislation coming in during 2007 may help to improve the situation.

IN SUMMARY

CHP is best suited to larger houses, often in combination with a supplementary heat source. It is easy to install and operate, achieves high levels of efficiency and some reductions in CO_2 emissions. But it cannot realistically make a big contribution to large-scale reductions in carbon emissions and long-term financial viablity must be in question.

1. CHP units offer efficiencies of up to 95 percent
2. On any fuel other than natural gas running costs tend to make them financially non-viable.
3. Installation is usually simple, especially as a replacement to an existing gas boiler.
4. Heating operation coincides with peak demand periods for electricity making the production of electricity virtually a by-product.
5. They are now known technology so exporting excess electricity to the National Grid is easy.
6. They are robust machines with a predicted lifespan of 15+ years.
7. CHP is not renewable energy as it runs on gas or oil. This also means that it inherently produces carbon emissions, although these are lower than the alternatives.
8. The viability is affected by fluctuating price of gas, oil and grid-generated electricity. It should also be noted that despite fairly extensive marketing, the Whispergen is still not available to the general market. The only currently available option is the Dachs-Senertec.

3

2. GENERATING ELECTRICITY

WIND TURBINES

There are only two issues related to selecting a wind turbine: size and location.

If you want to work out the size of the wind turbine you need from base principles then you may want to read The Green Building Bible, Volume 2 or The 40 percent House. They have all the information you need to carry out a reasonably accurate calculation on wind speed and swept diameter to probable power output. In the real world there is limited choice available to the domestic user and you may as well limit your calculations to those that you can buy.

To calculate the size of your wind turbine you will need to know your actual electrical consumption per year. The simplest way is to look at your electricity bill. It will show the number of units or kWh you use. Alternatively read the meter and measure what you actually use in the course of the year – don't calculate and don't rely on estimated bills.

Electricity consumption tends to attribute to the people in the house, rather than the house itself. So even if you are moving to a spanking new house, your electricity consumption will be broadly the same.

To give a view as to the margin of difference, a typical three to four-bedroom house with four people in occupation, using all incandescent light fittings and ageing electrical appliances will use 7,000kWh to 8,000kWh per year. Move those same people into a new house with all low energy lighting and A+ rated appliances and the consumption could fall to 5,000kWh to 6,000kWh. A substantial reduction in consumption and CO_2 emissions but not enough to materially affect the selection of the wind turbine.

You also need to decide on the proportion that you wish to generate. Again this can vary from, realistically, 30 percent to 200 percent. Once you have done that calculation you will find that you are limited to a choice of two or three wind turbines, perhaps four if you look hard enough.

Manufacturer's power output figures are usually based on a wind speed of 12 metres per second (m/s) or around 30mph. And while they are not inaccurate, they may be a bit misleading. Drive your car at 30mph and pop your hand out of the window to feel the effect. 30mph is a strong wind, much stronger than the UK experiences on a daily basis. A more common average wind speed is 5m/s to 6m/s or 10mph.

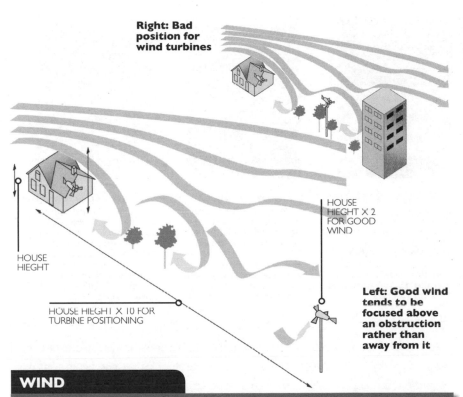

Right: Bad position for wind turbines

HOUSE HIEGHT × 2 FOR GOOD WIND

HOUSE HIEGHT

HOUSE HIEGHT × 10 FOR TURBINE POSITIONING

Left: Good wind tends to be focused above an obstruction rather than away from it

WIND

Wind force	Metres / second	MPH	Description	Effect
0	0 to 0.5	0 to 1	Calm	Smoke rises vertically
1	0.5 to 1.2	1 to 3	Light air	Smoke drifts but wind vanes not moved
2	1.2 to 3	4 to 7	Light breeze	Wind felt on face, leaves rustle
3	3 to 5	8 to 12	Gentle breeze	Leaves and twigs in motion, wind extends flags
4	5 to 8	13 to 18	Moderate breeze	Raises dust and paper; small branches move
5	8 to 10	19 to 24	Fresh breeze	Small trees in leaf sway, crested wavelets in inland water
6	10 to 13	15 to 31	Strong breeze	Branches in motion, whistling in telephone wires, umbrella used with difficulty
7	13 to 16	32 to 38	Near gale	Whole trees in motion; difficulty walking against the wind

The highlighted figures show the band within which wind turbines are typically rated and it is clear that it is not a common situation.

3

COURTESY SEGEN MICROGENERATION

COURTESY PROVEN ENERGY

Skystream 3.7. Rated at 1.8kW at wind speed of 12m/s. Potential production with average wind speed of 5.2m/s, 4000kWh p.a. (about the average domestic consumption). Price around £8,500 installed and connected.

Iskra AT5-1. Rated at 5kW at wind speeds of 12m/s. Potential production with average wind speed of 5m/s 8700kWh p.a. (about twice the annual average consumption. Price about £20,000 installed and connected.

Proven 2.5kW. Rated at 2.5kW at wind speeds of 12m/s. Potential production with average wind speed of 5m/s 5400kWh p.a. (about the annual average consumption. Price about £13,000 installed and connected.

As an example a 1kW rated wind turbine (similar to the one sold in your local DIY shed) will produce 1kW at 12m/s but at 6m/s it will produce just 125W – one eighth of its rated output. In urban locations the wind speed is slowed by all the roof tops and becomes more turbulent. The affect of this is that a wind that starts out at 6m/s will slow to 4m/s or even 3m/s by the time it gets to the town centre and our 1kW wind turbine will be producing next to nothing.

The DTI provide a wind speed database (at www.dti.gov.uk/energy/sources/renewables/renewables-explained/wind-energy/page27326.html). This will indicate the annual average wind speed in a kilometre square around your property at various heights above ground level. It is a good place to start and will indicate whether it is worth going any further. A general rule is that if the DTI database indicates an average wind speed of less than 5m/s it is unlikely to be productive. Less than 4m/s and it definitely won't. Over 6m/s and it is looking good for a turbine.

The wind speed on any site can vary significantly across very small distances. As little as 10m can bring the turbine out of the wind-shadow of a tree or building and into clean air. Raising the turbine 5m on a taller mast can have the same effect.

An effective wind turbine will cost between £5,000 and

£20,000. Investing £300 and perhaps three months in testing the wind speed and finding the best location would seem to make sense. Even if the DTI database is indicating strong potential, a 'Wind Prospector' from Windandsun Ltd (www.windandsun.co.uk) will indicate wind speed and direction across time and give an almost definitive guide as to the potential power.

PLANNING CONSENT

Wind turbines always need planning permission. The legislation is changing to make it easier (and cheaper) to obtain, but it is still needed. Some suppliers provide all the technical information, noise data, sizes, schematic drawings etc that are needed for a planning application, but not all. A good supplier can also provide information on other installations to support an application. These can significantly shorten the application process and reduce the cost.

The turbines illustrated here are typical for a domestic installation. There are many other available and which is best will depend on location, wind speed and budget.

In summary

1. Check before you buy. Wind is fickle and a small investment in checking speed and direction can save huge sums.
2. If you have neighbours, you need their approval. A single objector is often enough to kill a planning application (although the legislation is changing to help overcome this).
3. Wind turbines in urban locations do not justify their cost or their embodied CO_2
4. Wind turbines fixed to the house are less efficient than a wind turbine on a mast.
5. The bigger the turbine the better the return – £9,000 will buy a 2kW rated turbine producing maybe 4,000kWh pa. £15,000 will buy a 5kW turbine producing maybe 12,000kWh pa, (which will save about 5 tonnes of CO_2 each year!)
6. Wind turbines are not as noisy as you think. What is an acceptable noise level is a very personal matter and the only way to check if it is acceptable to you is to go and see one.
7. Flicker is often a bigger problem than noise. That is when the turbine blades either pass across the sun or reflect the sunlight, causing a flickering effect that may not be noticeable to the owner but may annoy neighbours. Again, location is the key and relating the prevailing wind to the path of the sun will indicate if flicker is likely to be a problem.
8. Equipment has a long life – 20+years – with a low, often DIY, maintenance requirement.

SOLAR CENTURY

PV technology is changing. As well as standard silicon cells, now we have PV arrays that look like roof slates and thick-film systems that replace the roof covering.

PHOTOVOLTAIC CELLS

Sometimes called solar panels and easily confused with solar thermal panels. Solar thermal panels produce hot water, while a PV cell generates electricity by allowing light to pass through a silicon crystal. Because of its atomic structure an electronic charge naturally moves around inside the crystal, but in a random manner. Arsenic and boron are added to the silicon and these impurities cause negative and positive molecules to join and encourage the flow of an electric charge in a single direction. Bombarding the molecules with sunlight causes electrons to be released, increasing the electric current which can be harvested. If you need to know more details of how they work and how they are made, read Richard J Komp's *Practical Photovoltaics*.

Photovoltaic cells have been produced on a large scale for over 40 years and have benefited from a significant amount of research and development, that continues today. BP's most recent product achieved a 4 percent improvement in conversion rates. This may not sound much but overall efficiency is only about 12 percent.

Taking our standard house, we need to generate 5,000kWh pa to power it. Using PV alone we would need an array of nearly 7kW rating to do it. In the UK, a 1kW rated PV array will generate between 750kWh and 850kWh per year depending on location and installation efficiencies. Therefore, divide 5,000 by 750 and you get to 7kW.

That equates to 0.75kWh per 1w rating for the UK. By comparison, in Arizona they get around 5kWh per year per 1w rating. Where you are in the world has a huge impact on the viablity of PV.

PV is the most expensive renewable energy option. Current prices for PV vary from £4,000 to £6,000 per kW installed.

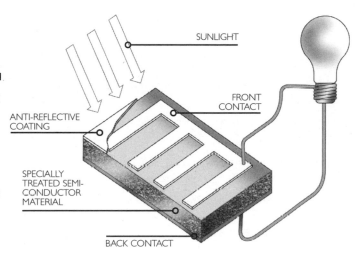

3

PV (photovoltaic solar panels generate electricity by the Photovoltaic Effect, discovered in 1839 by the 19yr old Edmund Becquerel. The photovoltaic effect is the phenomenon that certain materials produce electric current when they are exposed to light. For traditional PV solar panels a semiconductor PN junction is manufactured in which two halves of one pure silicon crystal are coated with two different materials (eg. arsenic, boron, aluminium, phosphorus). One half of the crystal is left electron deficient (the positive-type layer), and one half is left with an excess of electron (the negative-type layer). The coating on the silicon lead to an electric field across the junction between the two halves of the crystal with electrons able to travel in one direction only – from the electron rich half to the electron poor half.

SUNLIGHT

FRONT CONTACT

ANTI-REFLECTIVE COATING

SPECIALLY TREATED SEMI-CONDUCTOR MATERIAL

BACK CONTACT

For our standard house we would need to spend at least £28,000 on PV to generate the power needed. Buying that electricity from the grid would cost about £600 per year, which gives a simple pay-back of 46 years. But the system would save a little over two tonnes of CO_2 per year.

There are three basic types of PV cells, monocrystalline, polycrystalline and amorphous crystal. As the name suggests the monocrystaline is made from a single silicon crystal, polycrystalline from many crystals, amorphous cells are made from thousands of crystals.

Essentially, monocrystalline are more efficient and most expensive. Polycrystalline are less efficient and less expensive, amorphous are very inefficient and very cheap. Amorphous are the ones used in calculators, watches and the like and are cheaper to produce than the batteries they replace. But with efficiency ratings of around 5 percent they offer no practical solution at domestic or commercial scale. A lot of research is being done in this area, especially by the Chinese and efficiency is said to be up to 7.5 percent now. The word is that they are waiting until they break the 10 percent barrier before launching products on the market.

These may sound like very low efficiency rates but the best monocrystalline are only

3

achieveing efficiencies of 15 percent. The industry has been saying for many years that the price of moncrystalline cells will not fall unless and until there is a significantly higher take up of product. Which rather flies in the face of actuallity which shows prices falling by up to 30 percent over the past three to four years. This fall in price is largely due to the incursion of Chinese manufacturers into the market and has not prevented BP, Kyocera, Sony, Sharp and other huge multi-national companies investing millions in R&D.

PV systems are seeing a better take-up in commercial buildings where the extra cost of PV is considerably lower. A IKW array at £4,000 equates to a cost of £500 per m². If a prestige wall covering costs £300 per m² then the on cost is only £200 per m² or £1,600 per KW. The simple payback falls from 46 years to under 18 years. If and when these same economics can be applied to houses, PV will become a viable option for the home owner.

PV arrays, as in the first illustration, are typically fitted on top of the roof covering as they need freely circulating air to keep them cool. Conversion efficiency falls as the temperature of the cell rises above 25°C. New products are emerging, like the second photo which shows PV cells formed to match roof tiles or the third, which is a glass free PV panel which makes it very thin and very flexible. These work well in low light conditions inherent to cloudy climates and low-pitch roof angles.

All PV systems produce 12v electricity which has to pass through an inverter and control panel to convert it to 240v AC electricity for use in the home. All the reputable installers deal with this at the time of the installation and the cost is included in the rate per kW. Many suppliers will quote a diminishing price per kW for larger systems. This is because the fixed costs for the likes of control systems, scaffolding to get on the roof, turning up on site, remain the same for a 1kW system or 10kW system. So the bigger the system you buy, the cheaper it gets.

In summary

1. Once the system is installed it is maintenance free and will produce a consistent amount of electricity throughout its life.

2. Systems are supplied as modular panels and are easily scaleable to the electrical demand.

3. High capital cost can be offset if panels are used to substitute roofing or cladding materials.

4. Overall price/performance improves if used in conjunction with wind or hydro power.

5. Grid export is easy but necessary, as generation is typically not usually coincidental with use.

HYDRO POWER

3

Hydro is the granddaddy of renewable energy and if you have a stream with some head you really need to think about it. Modern Pelton wheel and Turgo turbines can trace their antecedence to Roman times. The physics has not changed although the technology has moved on a bit. They still work in basically the same way – 24 hours a day, seven days a week. Water is passed over a wheel, producing torque (rotation) energy.

The key issues are head – the vertical distance between the highest and lowest points of the stream – and flow – the amount of water passing a point, measured in litres per second.

Measuring the stream to assess the potential looks a complicated business and experts charge a lot of money to do it for you. It is quite possible to measure it yourself and get accurate enough to decide if it is worth investing in an expert to do it properly.

The first thing is to establish if you own both banks of the stream. If not you will need the express, legal consent of the person who owns the other bank. You will be making a substantial investment in a hydro turbine that is likely to generate an annual income. The existing owner of the other bank may be a perfectly nice person and happy for you to do what you want. The person he sells his property to may not be so nice.

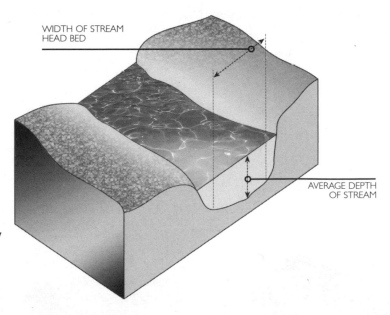

WIDTH OF STREAM
HEAD BED

AVERAGE DEPTH
OF STREAM

Measuring flow will tell you if the garden stream is up to generating hydro-electric power.

3

If you own both banks, start with measuring the head. Head is the vertical distance from the top of the stream to the bottom. Typically, you will not own the whole of the stream so only measure the bit you own.

The easiest way is to buy a large scale OS map and find your bit of the stream on it. The contour lines will then tell you the height the stream falls.

Alternatively invest in a little altimeter.

We are ideally looking for head of more than 10m. With a fairly small flow 10m head will generate a reasonable amount of power. It is quite possible to use streams with lower heads – down to as little as 2m – but the more head the more power to be obtained from it.

Measuring flow is a more complex business if it is to be done accurately. The time of year and the recent rainfall are likely to affect the amount of water in the stream and therefore the flow rate. The flow rate is likely to be different in January to June. It is possible to estimate the flow rate across the year, and hydro experts typically have access to the necessary data to do it, but the only way to get accurate figures is to measure the flow at different time of the year.

There are two methods of getting a rough estimate of the flow rate.

The first was set out by AA Milne in House at Pooh Corner – playing Pooh sticks. Find a reasonably clear stretch of the stream, the longer the better but at least a 2m long stretch. Place two markers on the bank of the stream at a known (and convenient) distance apart, drop a stick in the stream at the upstream marker and time how long the stick takes to reach the downstream marker. Repeat until bored. Average out the results and that will give a figure in metres per second.

Next measure the size of the stream, which may involve wellies. Measure the width of the stream (at the point you played Pooh sticks) and its average depth. These figures do not have to be spot on, but the more accurate the better.

Let's assume that a sample stream is 600mm wide and 75mm average depth, and that it flows at a rate of 0.5m per second.

> **To calculate the stream flow rate:**
> 600mm x 75mm = 0.045m²
> 0.045 × 0.5 (m/sec) = 0.0225 m³ per second
> 1m³ = 1000 litres, therefore 0.0225m³ = 22.5 litres per second flow rate in the sample stream.

3

An alternative method, if there is any sort of waterfall in the stream, is to find a container (bucket, tub, barrel – bigger the better), measure its capacity in litres, place it under the fall and time how long it takes to fill. That will also give a figure in litres per second. Again, repeat until bored and average the results.

With those two figures – head and flow rate – it is possible to calculate the potential power in the stream.

The calculations is:

Head × flow rate × gravity × 0.7 system inefficiencies

For our sample stream the calculation is:

$10 \times 22.5 \times 9.81 \times 0.7 = 1545$ watts of power.

1.5kW may not sound much compared to, say, a 5kW wind turbine but a 1.5kW hydro turbine will produce 1.5kW 24 hours per day, every day. It will generate at least 12,000kWh per year and our standard house needs just 5,000kWh per year, leaving 7,000 to be sold to the grid.

In reality, the flow rate of most stream is likely to vary across the year – more rain in winter, more water in the stream. A well-designed hydro system will account for this by building in different nozzles to optimise the power potential to the flow of the stream.

Another factor is that it is unwise, as well as unlawful, to use all the water in the stream. The stream is an ecosystem that relies on the water. Removing it will kill the ecosystem. In all cases the Environment Agency needs to be contacted to advise as to what is a reasonable amount to extract but it is unlikely to be more than half. So in our sample case we would be thinking of installing a 0.75kW turbine, which will generate enough power to meet the demands of our standard house.

Typical hydro Installation

A typical installation needs:

1. Water intake – to divert the flow from the water course to the turbine. This will also incorporate a trash guard and a fish guard. Both essential elements of the system.
2. A 'penstoke' – which is usually a pipe to carry the water from the intake to the turbine. The diameter and material are critical to ensure head pressure is maintained and contained.
3. A 'powerhouse' – a grand name for what is usually a simple and small box constructed from concrete blocks.
4. An outflow – to ensure the water gets back to the stream with no pressure build-up in the turbine.
5. Control system to move the electricity generated to the point of use.

3

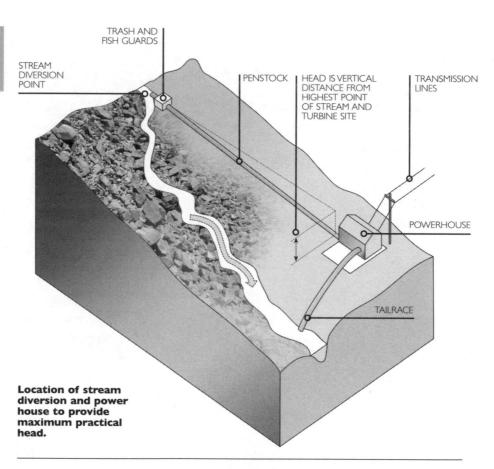

STREAM
DIVERSION
POINT

TRASH AND
FISH GUARDS

PENSTOCK

HEAD IS VERTICAL
DISTANCE FROM
HIGHEST POINT
OF STREAM AND
TURBINE SITE

TRANSMISSION
LINES

POWERHOUSE

TAILRACE

**Location of stream
diversion and power
house to provide
maximum practical
head.**

TYPES OF TURBINE INSTALLATION

There are two types of water turbines: Impulse and Reaction. The best way to understand the basic difference is to imagine yourself on roller skates and someone turns a fire hose on you. Your movement under this condition would be 'impulse'. Now suppose that you were handed the fire hose. Your movement under this condition would be 'reaction'. The Pelton, Turgo, Crossflow and Kaplan are impulse turbines, deriving their power from turning, slowing or stopping the flow of water striking their blades. The Francis, Leffel, and Fourneyron are reaction turbines, deriving their power from the reactive force of the water passing between their blades.

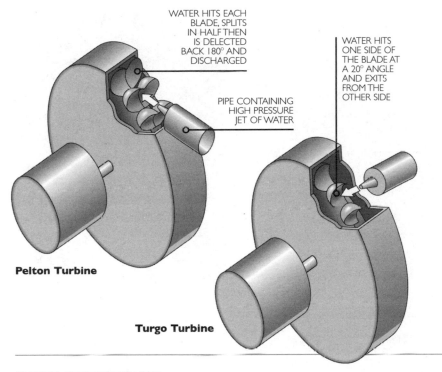

WATER HITS EACH
BLADE, SPLITS
IN HALF THEN
IS DEFLECTED
BACK 180° AND
DISCHARGED

WATER HITS
ONE SIDE OF
THE BLADE AT
A 20° ANGLE
AND EXITS
FROM THE
OTHER SIDE

PIPE CONTAINING
HIGH PRESSURE
JET OF WATER

Pelton Turbine

Turgo Turbine

IMPULSE TURBINES

The *Pelton Turbine* is common for micro-hydro and is made up of a wheel with a series of blades, each of which is a split bucket. A high pressure jet of water is directed at the blades and as the jet hits each blade it is split in half, so that each half is turned and deflected back almost 180°. Up to 90 percent of the energy of the water goes into propelling the blade and the deflected water falls out of a discharge channel.

The Turgo turbine is equally common and very similar to the Pelton. In this case, the jet strikes the plane of the blade at typically 20° angle so that the water enters the runner on one side and exits on the other. In this way, the flow rate is not limited by the discharged fluid interfering with the incoming jet (as is the case with Pelton turbines). As a consequence, a Turgo turbine will have a smaller diameter rotor than a Pelton for an equivalent power.

Both Pelton and Turgo turbines need a reasonably good head to produce the pressure necessary to generate power. In both cases, the diameter of the jet nozzle can be varied to cope with different rates of flow to accommodate variations across the year. This can be a manual change of the nozzle, or more sophisticated systems can automate the switch.

3

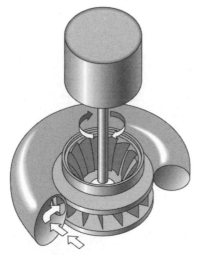

The Francis Spiral-case turbine.

REACTION TURBINES

The most common reaction turbine in micro-hydro installation is the Francis turbine, which is a good option for low-head schemes.

To work well the water needs to be given a spin as it enters the turbine. This is done either in the casing or in the intake.

The best source of information on all types of hydro turbines – large and small – is the British Hydro Association at www.british-hydro.org

Costs

The down side of hydro power is that the cost can vary from the sublime to the ridiculous. For our sample stream a 0.75kW turbine alone can vary in price from £600 to £6,000 depending on supplier, manufacturer and type of turbine. The generator and control equipment can similarly vary from £2,500 to £5,000. These are the known elements. The unknown elements are the costs associated with capturing the water and delivering it to the turbine. These vary with every installation, as every stream is different. And some suppliers charge considerably more for this element than others.

The good news is that there are few big players in the domestic-scale hydro market. It is serviced largely by an increasing number of small businesses run by enthusiasts.

By way of illustration, if we assume that the capital cost of our example 0.75kW system is £10,000, a cost analysis would show:

Capital cost	**= £10,000**
Output	**= 6,525 kWh pa**
System life	**= 30 years**
Maintenance cost	**= £200 pa**
Total life cost	**= £16,000**
Whole life output	**= 195,750 kWh**
Cost per kWh	**= 8.1p per kWh**

While 8.1p per unit may not sound much better than the 11p price from the grid, bear in mind that the 8.1p is fixed for 30 years. The 11p is quite likely to rise.

Payback on renewable energy is a moot point (as you will read elsewhere), but in this case it is a reasonable measure of the financial viability of the scheme, and of the potential supplier. Any worthwhile hydro scheme needs to recover its capital cost in less than seven years. Less than five years is often achievable and any proposal that pushes the figures beyond that needs careful consideration.

The Environment Agency (EA) is, together with the National Rivers Agency, responsible for every river and stream in the country. It is essential that the EA is contacted in every case. There is a legal requirement to obtain an Abstraction Licence and pay the necessary fee (although you may well ask why you need to pay a fee to use the water in a stream you already own!), which will vary with the size of the scheme but will be in the order of hundreds of pounds. The total cost of obtaining an Abstraction Licence will be £1,500 to £3,000 depending on the size of the scheme, followed by an annual fee of £140 upwards, again depending on the size of the scheme.

There is also a moral obligation to ensure that the scheme does not damage the ecology, and the EA are the right people to advise on this. Generally their advice is good, well intentioned and free.

Noise can be an issue with hydro power, more so than wind. Water is moving at relatively high pressure across a spinning wheel of some sort. It is bound to generate noise. Unlike wind, however, the hydro turbine will be contained in a plant room. This may be as small as 1.5m x 1.5m x 1m but is sufficient to contain most of the noise as well as the kit.

3

Planning consent may be an issue. Always speak to the local planning authority, but typically they are only interested in the plant room and, if that is small, they are usually happy to grant consent or allow construction on a building notice.

In summary

1. Pound for pound, hydro will produce more electricity than any other technology.
2. The cost will vary hugely with the scheme but should always recover its cost in under five years.
3. Modern equipment is highly resilient and should comfortably have a life of 10 to 20 years.
4. Designing and installing hydro schemes is expert work, but establishing if it is worthwhile can be done by the amateur.

ELECTRICITY STORAGE

Electricity is produced when the sun shines (or when there is a reasonable amount of daylight to be more accurate. Electricity will be produced on cloudy days, just not so much), or when the wind blows or the stream flows. We want most of the electricity in the evening when conditions may not be right and our system is not generating. In addition, our hyrdro turbine may be 0.75kW output, or the wind turbine 2.5kW and if we have a few appliances running, there is just not enough power available. But the hydro turbine will run 24-7 and the wind turbine all the time the wind blows and either will produce enough energy across the year for the demands of the house.

So we need to store the electricity we generate until we want to use it. The most practical option is to use the electricity in the house when you can and export to the grid when you can't. This is the cheapest option and the connection needed (called a G83 connection) is well known and recognised through out the PV and grid-generating industry. It should be noted that G83 is limited to an export capacity of 16 amps per phase, or 3.8kW maximum capacity. This is a fairly arbitrary figure and usually extended to 4kW. Generators above that capacity need a different connection system, called G59, which tends to be purpose-built and consequently more expensive.

A net-metering system will be needed and is obtained from the electricity supplier (Npower, Swalec, Manweb, Scottish & Southern, etc) although some are less keen than others. It pays to shop around if you are considering any form of micro generation. Good Energy are well set-up for micro-generators and very helpful. Net metering is in effect two electricity meters, one measuring the electricity coming into the house from the grid and the other measuring the electricity going out. The consumer pays, or is paid, for the difference. In this way it is possible to 'store' generated electricity on the grid for later use at no cost.

Batteries are sometimes used for storage when grid connection is not available. These need to be deep-cycle batteries to be able to put up with the charge and discharge cycle typical in micro generation. Deep-cycle batteries are expensive and will add maybe £2,000 to the cost of the installation. They will have a life of perhaps 10 years, compared to 40+ years for the PVs.

3. GENERATING HEAT

BIOMASS

By biomass we mean anything that was grown and can be used as fuel. It is most often wood, in the form of logs, chips or pellets, but also includes wood dust briquettes, straw bale or pellet, rape seed pellets, wheat and miscanthus pellets. It is still something of an emerging technology in the UK, but is well established across central and northern Europe. In 2005, 85 percent of all new homes built in Austria had wood pellet boilers installed as standard.

Biomass is virtually carbon neutral, the CO_2 produced as a result of combustion being no more than the CO_2 absorbed while it was growing. There is an issue to do with harvesting, processing and transport, which all add to the carbon footprint, but it still has the lowest real-terms affect on CO_2 emissions.

Efficiencies in modern biomass boilers can be high, up to 92 percent, but care has to be taken with selecting boilers to match the fuel. A few boilers will burn multiple fuels, but most are designed specifically for a particular fuel type. Some are capable of burning multiple fuels but are set up at the time of installation to burn a particular fuel or to burn that fuel most efficiently. Most of the biomass boilers you see are wood pellet boilers, but that doesn't necessarily mean that wood pellet is the best idea. Fuel supply is still very much a local issue as there is no nationwide network of supply. What is available in your area, reliably and at a good price, will influence which system you buy.

A point to consider is that the Government has decreed that as of 2008, 5 percent of diesel road fuel must come from a renewable source. The automotive fuels industry has decided that will be principally rape-seed oil because they can mix 5 percent rape oil with diesel without any noticeable change to the performance of the engine. When oil is extracted from rape seed, it leaves a residue called 'cake', which is a biomass fuel with a good calorific

3

value (you gets lots of heat from it). A mix of 5 percent may not seem much, but spread across the nation (and the whole of Europe) it is a lot of rape seed cake. What effect that will have on the price of rape seed pellet is yet to be seen, but it will at least put a lot more potential fuel on the market.

In addition, that 5 percent mix is set to rise to 20 percent over the next few years, meaning there is likely to be a lot of rape seed cake about. Whether that gets turned into pellets is yet to be seen, but it might.

The manual labour involved in biomass can have an impact. Biomass boiler systems can be highly automated, but none of them are free of some labour input. At the lowest level the user will have to empty ash from the boiler, perhaps as infrequently as every three months. At the other end of the scale, the batch log boilers require the user to load logs and empty the ash, usually on a daily basis. There are various steps in between and when you are buying a biomass boiler you need a clear understanding of the work you will have to put in.

THE BIOMASS FUEL MARKET

A Royal Commission report in 2006 into the potential UK Biomass Market stated that biomass already provides approximately 60 percent of total EU renewable energy utilisation and is therefore the most mature and commercially viable renewable technology in the EU.

The Forestry Commission estimates that the sawmill co-product (dust and offcuts) available in Britain totals around 859,000 oven-dried tones per year, 20 percent of which is sawdust, available for pelleting. There are existing markets for most of this resource, but the Forestry Commission estimates that around half the sawdust could be made available for fuel without serious disruption to existing industries.

The only figures we have on biomass prices comparisons are produced by Strathclyde University (not surprisingly, Scotland is very interested in wood fuels).

Price Comparison (As at November 2006)	
Electricity	4.5 to 12.6p/kWh
Heating oil (in condensing boiler)	5.2p/kWh
LPG (in condensing boiler)	6.7p/kWh
Coal (anthracite grains)	3.5p/kWh
Natural gas	3.5p/kWh
Logs in stove	0 to 5.1p/kWh
Wood chips	2 to 2.5p/kWh
Wood pellet	3.2 to 3.8p/kWh

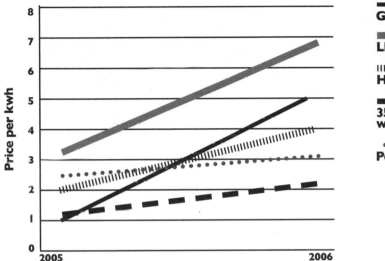

Gas

LPG

Heating Oil

35%mc woodchip

Pellets

Price Changes 2005 – 2006 Compared to Fossil Fuels

The graphs show that while wood chip and wood pellet prices have both risen, the rise is much slower than fossil fuels and that, in fact, the rise can be attributed to the increased transport cost brought about by the rise in road fuel prices.

FUEL STORAGE

Unlike other renewable energy technologies, biomass fuel has to be stored on site. And it can be quite bulky. A conventionally insulated house (ie built to current building regs) will require seven to eight tonnes of biomass a year. The storage capacity needed will vary with the fuel (wood chip is a lot bulkier than wood pellet) and the frequency of delivery. For guidance six tonnes of wood pellet is around 10m³ which could easily double or even treble for wood chip.

A typical delivery would be two or three tonnes so a bulk storage of 4m³ or 5m³ would be typical if you are using pellet. That can be either a proprietary system, like those on the next page, or a purpose-built store. In either case, a delivery system is also needed to move the fuel from the store to the boiler.

Most biomass boilers have an on-board fuel hopper that can be loaded by hand. These

3

WWW.ORGANICENERGY.CO.UK
WWW.HIGHLANDWOODENERGY.CO.UK

Above: two types of pellet-storage system. Right: Extraflame pellet stove with back boiler, and the on-board hopper being loaded.

can be just a few litres capacity or up to several hundred litres, depending on the boiler.

For full automation (or as close as can be) a fuel store is necessary. Okofen and KWB machines shown are the more automated options and a complete system, including fuel store, fuel delivery system and installation could cost £12,000. But taking on the burden of loading by hand makes major cost savings. The illustration below shows an Extraflame pellet stove with back boiler, and the on-board hopper being loaded.

The hopper will hold around 20kg of wood pellet, which is handily delivered in 18kg or 20kg bags. Depending on the time of year and the level of use, one hopper load could last three or four days. This system would cost around £3,000.

GROW YOUR OWN FUEL

For the more enthusiastic among us the potential exists to grow your own fuel. You will need around two hectares or five acres of land and the will power and energy to plant, harvest and process the crop.

A good plantation will have a mix of coppice and short rotation crops, so a mix of willow, hazel, alder, ash and possibly miscanthus. This will not only encourage all sorts of flora and fauna but will give a crop every year from year two.

The cheapest and most effective use of home-grown fuel is as wood chip as the process equipment needed is just a shredder. The crop needs to be dried before it is processed or burnt and typically the wood is cut, left to dry for three to six months, shredded and left a further three months. This will get moisture content below 20 percent and this regime of dry-shred-dry again is used for a couple of reasons. If the wood is shredded wet it will have to be turned regularly to avoid it composting. Shredding the wood dry puts more strain on the shredder and shortens the life of the blades. Partial drying first is a happy compromise.

Storage becomes even more of a issue but if you have five acres of spare land then you probably have room for a fuel store.

In Summary
1. Biomass is a direct replacement to oil or gas-fired boilers.
2. It is effectively carbon neutral.
3. The cost of fuel is rising on a much flatter curve than fossil fuels.
4. Availability of biomass fuels is still not good, but is improving every year.
5. Local availability of a reliable source of fuel is key to a reliable installation.
6. Biomass fuel has to be stored on site and fuel stores can be big and expensive.

4. HEAT PUMPS

There are a number of different types of heat pumps but they all use the compressor technology of the refrigerator to move heat from one place to another. They do not, or should not, generate heat. Heat pumps work by collecting heat from air, water or the ground, using compression and expansion to, in effect, magnify the heat and transfer it to water or air.

Because the technology 'magnifies' the heat, the less they have to magnify the more efficient they are. That is, the closer the source temperature and the required temperature are the more efficient the heat pump. The ground below 1m deep remains at a fairly constant 7°C to 12°C throughout the year. We want a temperature of 21°C in the house. That is a temperature difference of 14°C to 9°C. That presents are known and quantifiable limits for heat pump manufacturers to work with. Machinery can be designed to optimum levels to work extremely efficiently within those relatively close parameters. External air, on the other hand, can vary in temperature from -5°C to 25°C giving a potential temperature difference of 26°C.

Manufacturers of heat pumps advertise their wares as having a coefficient of productivity (COP) that will typically be 3, 4 or 5. This means that for every 1kW of electricity you put in, you will get 3, 4 or 5 kWs of heat out. It is calculated by the manufacturer based on the optimum input and output temperatures. The output temperature is the critical factor and will generally be between 30° and 40°C. This is to minimise the temperature difference and

3

achieve a reasonable COP. It is not accidental that 30^0 and 40^0C are good operating temperatures for underfloor heating. Radiators need temperatures over 55^0C and hot water needs to be stored at 65^0C to avoid Legionnaires disease.

Forcing air and ground source heat pumps up to 50^0C or 60^0C significantly reduces efficiency, in some cases bringing the COP down to two. To overcome this, some manufacturers install what are effectively immersion heaters in the machine. So a heat pump rated at 12kW may actually be a 6kW heat pump with 6kW of immersion heaters. The manufacturer can then, in all honesty, claim that it has 12kW output and a COP of 4. The fact that the two don't come together need not be said.

Irrespective of whether the heating distribution is underfloor or radiators, the fact is that domestic hot water needs to be stored at 65^0C. How that temperature is achieved is a different question, but so far as the heat pump is concerned, buyers need to ask sellers what the COP will be at 65^0C. And if the buyer is told that the COP is the same at 65^0C as at 45^0C they probably need to look for another seller.

The most cost-effective option is to have two separate systems, one for space heating and another for hot water. The heat pump driving underfloor heating will be working at relatively low temperatures and at peak efficiency. The hot water system can be heated by solar panels or, if budget doesn't allow, by immersion heaters on off-peak electricity tariff (Economy 7).

Mixing heat pumps and immersion heaters in the same machine means that at times of peak heat load (winter) the immersion heaters will be used as a primary heat source, with the consequent impact on the electricity bill. To return to the opening statement, heat pumps move heat from one place to another. They should not generate heat.

GROUND SOURCE HEAT PUMPS

The first ground source heat pump (GSHP) installed in the UK went into the Royal Festival Hall in 1951 and it is by far the most popular form of heat pump. It is about to become even more so with manufacturers like Worcester-Bosch and Dimplex entering the market in a big way.

GSHPs use an array of pipes in a closed loop buried in the ground as heat collectors. Pipes can be either straight or slinky and both operate by pumping a cooled fluid through the pipes, absorbing the heat in the ground and extracting the collected heat via a heat exchanger.

There is no material difference in whether straight or slinky pipes are used as the machine will be configured to work best with that type of pipe. In both case the machine will

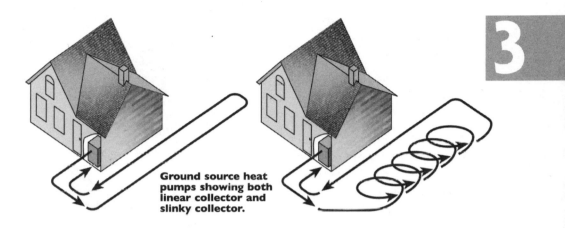

Ground source heat pumps showing both linear collector and slinky collector.

need a 10m length of pipe for each 1kW output. So that a 10kW heat pump will want a 100m pipe run.

Again in both cases the pipes will need to be buried in trenches 1m to 1.5m deep. Different machines require different minimum depths. In all cases 1.5m to 2m deep ensures a more constant source temperature. But new health and safety regulations stipulate that trenches over 1.2m must have trench shuttering to prevent trench collapse, increasing the cost of the installation.

The pipes also need to be spaced apart properly to ensure that each pipe is not robbing heat from the pipe next to it. In the case of a straight pipe this will be not less than 3m apart and slinkies not less than 5m apart. A 10kW heat pump using a slinky array will need 500m^2 of ground to accommodate it. Squeezing it into a smaller area will adversely impact on efficiency and increase the electricity bill.

Which is where the real impact of the heat pumps that incorporate immersion heaters is felt. If this type of system is undersized or squeezed into too small a ground area the immersion heaters take over sooner as the heat pump is unable to deliver the expected heat. The system is then running on a COP of 1 for at least 50 percent of its output and electricity bills will spiral out of control.

There are compact collectors available where the necessary ground area is not available and pipes can be arranged in multiple boreholes but these options add significantly to the capital cost, to the point where other technologies may offer a better option. Having said that, new products and ways of collecting heat pop up now and again and it is worth keeping an eye on the market.

3 WATER-SOURCE HEAT PUMPS

This uses the same basic idea as GSHP but has an open loop of pipes that take water from a source (stream, lake or borehole), extracts heat from it and returns the water to another stream, lake or borehole. (It can't go back to the same source because it will chill the water there.)

The illustration shows water being extracted from a borehole, passing through the heat pump and returned to a stream. This illustrates that the return water is as clean as it was when it came out of the borehole. If there is a good size stream that close, it would make more sense to take the water from the stream and return it slightly downstream.

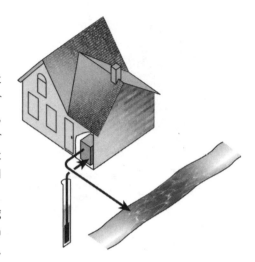

A water-source heat pump in action. Water is taken from a borehole, it passes through a pump in the house, the heat is extracted and then the water is returned to the stream.

Lakes can be used but the feed to the lake must be at least as much as the water being extracted or there is the potential to drain the lake.

The amount of water required is usually 1.5 litres per kW per minute. So our 10kW heat pump will need 15 litres of water each minute that it runs. Typical running time will be six hours per day so the system needs 5400 litres of water per day.

Water source heat pumps tend to operate at better COP than ground source, typically five instead of four, due to the high volume of source material. They also use superheat heat exchangers to raise the output temperature of a small volume of water over 65^0C.

Water source heat pumps most commonly use boreholes as the water source but this can add considerably to the capital cost. The cost of a borehole will vary enormously with the ground conditions, the depth to the water table and the amount of water needed. They are never cheap. The cost of mobilising borehole drilling equipment is high and remains the same whatever the depth of hole needed. Minimum cost will be £2,000 and it could be 10 times that much.

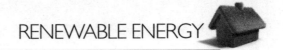

POWER SUPPLY

3

Both ground- and water-source heat pumps impose a heavy start-up load on the electricity supply. This load is for less than a second and has no implications in terms of the bill but usually has implications in terms of the supply itself.

The start-up load varies with the size of the heat pump and with the manufacturer, but can reach 65 or 70amps. Normal domestic supply is 80amps which means that if there is normal domestic activity going on in the house when the heat pump starts up, it will pop the fuse. Many manufacturers are installing soft-start motors to reduce the start-up load but buyers should always check what the start-up load for the particular model is, and if their existing supply can cope. If not, upgrading the supply can be expensive and a quote from the electricity supply company needs to be obtained before ordering the heat pump. Larger heat pumps, over 20kW, often require a three-phase supply, and again, quotes should be obtained from the electricity supplier before committing to the purchase of the heat pump. Installing a three-phase supply can cost from a few hundred pounds to several thousands.

AIR SOURCE HEAT PUMPS

There are two sorts: air-to-air and air-to-water.

Air-to-air are basically air conditioning machines operating the other way round. They have very low COP, maybe as little as 1.5 in winter, and tend to be small output, 1.5kW or 2kW is common. They are best used in small, isolated areas that have high solar heat gains so that they can serve the double function of heating and cooling. Put simply, in winter they blow out hot air and in summer cool air. At either end of the scale the COP is low and they are really only efficient in spring and autumn when the inside and outside air temperatures are closer. On the upside they are low capital cost items, £250 to £300 would be usual with DIY fitting quite practical.

Trianco market a range of air-to-water heat pumps that offer a COP of around three (the COP will vary through the year as the air temperature varies). These range from 3kW output to 17kW and although the COP is lower than GSHP, so is the price. At £3,500 for the largest model they are around half the price of the equivalent GSPH.

In Summary

1. Heat pumps are not strictly renewable energy as they run on electricity (unless you generate the electricity from a renewable source) but they are the most efficient way

3

of using non-renewable energy to heat the home.

2. If they are run on mains electricity they will increase the CO_2 emissions.

3. Sharp selling practices and insufficient ground space can lead to poorly-designed systems that become remarkably inefficient.

4. Water source is best, but only if there is a supply of water available. The need to drill a borehole can make the project too expensive.

5. Air source needs to be treated with caution. There are good air-to-water machines available but there are also very poor air-to-air machines.

6. With ground source, the cost and disturbance of the trench should not be overlooked. Heat pumps generally are robust, reliable technology. A properly designed and sized system needs no back-up system (gas or oil boiler) and, with proper servicing, will last 15 to 20 years. Heat pumps still cost more than a comparable gas- or oil-fired boiler but the price is falling and over the life of the machine, heat pumps will always save money.

SOLAR HOT WATER

A typical domestic solar hot water system of $3m^2$ to $4m^2$ will deliver 1,500 to 2,000kWh pa, providing about 70 percent of annual hot water needs and saving about 0.2 to 0.4 tonnes of carbon per annum. Once the system is installed there are no maintenance charges and no running costs. It will go on producing hot water for up to 40 years, maybe more. This is an area where there is most excitement about pay-back. A typical domestic system will cost £3,500 to £4,000 installed and will repay its cost in around 20 years, compared to generating the same heat from a gas boiler.

That may seem like a long time, but double glazing will cost in excess of £10,000 and pay-back will be more than 90 years in terms of the energy they save. Who would think about building a house without double glazing? How long will it be before solar hot water is accepted as the norm, as clearly it should be?

All solar panels work on the same principal of light passing through glass being refracted and generating heat. The heat is captured in a collector, usually water, and stored in a hot water cylinder. The cylinder needs to be bigger than the normal 80 litre copper cylinder as the system needs to store as much heat as possible while the sun shines – although, in fact, solar panels don't actually need sunshine. So long as there is light they produce heat. The more light, the more heat.

There are two kinds of solar panel for generating hot water:

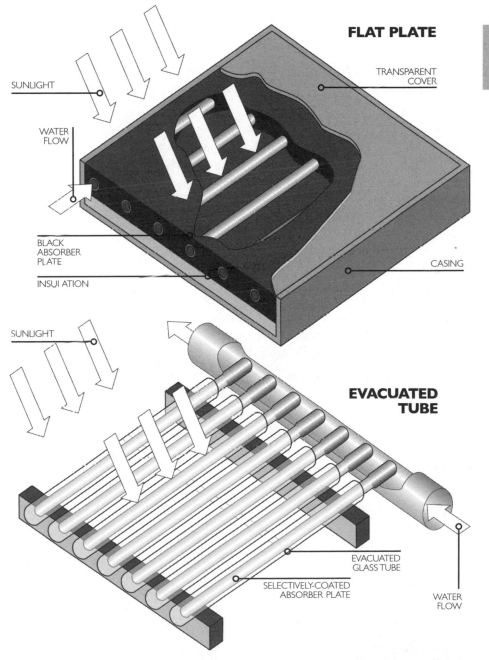

FLAT PLATE

3

SUNLIGHT

TRANSPARENT
COVER

WATER
FLOW

BLACK
ABSORBER
PLATE

INSULATION

CASING

SUNLIGHT

**EVACUATED
TUBE**

EVACUATED
GLASS TUBE

SELECTIVELY-COATED
ABSORBER PLATE

WATER
FLOW

3

flat plate and evacuated tube.

Flat plate is a box with pipes running through it covered by a flat glass or polycarbide plate. These can be used for roof integration (where they are mounted in the roof in place of the roof covering) as well as roof mounting (where they are mounted on top of the roof covering).

Evacuated tube are, as the name implies, a glass tube carrying a vacuum, similar to a thermos flask. They also have a pipe running down the middle with water in it to collect the heat and carry it to the hot water store. The evacuated tube system can only be roof mounted and is more fragile than flat plate. They are, therefore, not suited to mounting in places where they could come into contact with a cricket ball or falling branch.

There are lots of figures about the relative efficiencies of the two types. Manufacturers of each can prove conclusively that their product is more efficient than the competition. Evacuated tube are a bit more expensive and in some situations, notably when the roof is some degrees off south, can be more efficient. Flat panel are the only option for roof integration and should be used if there is any danger of breakage. The cost of repair is extremely high as it involves at least two people and scaffolding.

Solar panel technology has not changed in any significant way in 35 years. There is no reason for big variations in price, but nonetheless there are big variations. It is being seen as a quick fix for people who want to seem green and is being high-pressure sold in the same way that double glazing was 25 years ago. A 4m^2 flat panel installed on roof, including a 200-litre tank, all labour, peripheral parts and control systems should cost no more than £4,000. If the price you are quoted is significantly above that, find another supplier.

Planning consent

The laws relating to planning consent for solar panels is changing to make it easier to gain consent. In general, consent will always be granted except in conservation areas and on listed buildings. In these cases normal planning restrictions will apply and a case must be made for the grant of consent.

An issue to bear in mind is that roof integrated systems do not need specific planning consent if they project less than 120mm above the roof plane. In that case, it comes under permitted development rights (similar to erecting a TV aerial) and no consent is needed and no fee need be paid.

In summary

1. A good solar system will provide all the hot water in spring and summer and can contribute to space heating.
2. Solar thermal systems are simple, robust technology with extremely long life.
3. They are maintenance free and have extremely low running costs.
4. Siting to be south facing and to avoid shading is important to effectiveness.
5. Every home should have one.

3

GRANTS FOR RENEWABLE ENERGY

The Low Carbon Build Program is still providing grants for renewable energy technologies. Check out their web site at www.lowcarbonbuildings.org.uk for the latest details. At the time of going to press, the grants available were:

Technology	Maximum Amount of Gran
Solar photovoltaics	Maximum of £2,000 per kW of installed capacity, subject to an overall maximum
Wind turbines	Maximum of £1,000 per kW of installed capacity, subject to an overall maximum of £2,500 or 30% of the relevant eligible costs, whichever is the lower
Small hydro	Maximum of £1,000 per kW of installed capacity, subject to an overall maximum of £2,500 or 30% of the relevant eligible costs, whichever is the lower
Solar thermal hot water	Overall maximum of £400 or 30% of the eligible costs, whichever is the lower
Ground source heat pump	Overall maximum of £1,200 or 30% of the eligible costs, whichever is the lower
Automated wood pellet fed heaters/ stoves	Overall maximum of £600 or 20% of the eligible costs, whichever is the lower
Wood-fuelled boiler systems	Overall maximum of £1,500 or 30% of the relevant eligible costs, whichever is the lower

Applying is easy and fast but must be done online. Grants are guaranteed to be available into 2008, but will cease when the available fund of £30M is exhausted.

4 SUSTAINABLE MATERIALS

The case for using sustainable materials is a good one. 50 percent of material resources taken from nature are for buildings. 50 percent of waste production in the UK comes from the building industry. The biggest single source, 28 percent, of the CO_2 embodied in buildings is in the stone, sand and aggregates used. 82 percent of the material used in the conventional house is virgin material, and currently a huge proportion of that is from non-sustainable sources.

Our standard house will use some 200 tonnes of materials with up to 44 tonnes of CO_2 embodied in those materials. This carbon footprint calculation below is for an average UK house and has been calculated using data from BRE Wales. As this information was very general in its nature, it has been supplemented by referring to the Bath University Inventory of Carbon and Energy (ICE) data sheets. The 'average house' is assumed to be two storey, have a ground floor area of $72m^2$ ($140m^2$ overall), brick and block cavity wall on traditional foundations and concrete ground floor topped off with a concrete tile pitched roof.

This models the main structure of an 'average' house and so the figures are an extrapolation from quantities used across the UK. It takes the property to a weatherproof condition with painted walls, but does not account for decorative finishes, fixtures or fittings or landscaping. If we add a proportion for waste materials and CO_2 emitted during the construction process, the figure climbs to 54 tonnes.

A zero-carbon house – that is a house emitting zero carbon dioxide, as proposed by the Government for 2016 – that is conventionally built will take some nine years to recover the carbon dioxide embodied in it.

If the level of sustainability aimed at was to have only a timber-framed house, faced with reclaimed brick with reclaimed slates on the roof and everything else new, non-sustainable material, the house would reduce its embodied carbon by almost 12 tonnes.

MATERIALS

4

Resource	Quantity per house	Kg CO_2 per house	Comments
Spoil	12m³	750	
Blocks	1,586	6,823	High density concrete
Bricks	6,940	4,164	3kg brick
Reinforced beams	26m	800	
Plasterboard	148m²	180	Weight taken from COSHH sheets
Mortar	3m³	690	
Glass	27m²	2,109	Based on UPVC double glazing.
Timber	6m3	1,096	At 400kg/m³
Paint	75ltr	457	Acrylic paint
Roadway	52m²	16,783	Concrete with tarmac over
Concrete roof tile	93m²	2,700	Data from the BRE elemental tables
Concrete floor	72m²	1,173	
General insulation	500kg (estimated)	1,303	Assumes polyurethane foam
Membrane	80m² 8kg	66	Assumes plastic sheet, 120 microns
Ancillaries		5,000	Wiring, pipes, drainage etc.
Total CO^2		**43,914**	

Sustainability starts from the point of reducing the drain on natural resources and clearly considering what materials to use is a fundamental part of that. Ten years ago a sustainable building was a bit of a strange beast. People that built them were dedicated souls fighting almost insurmountable problems. The sustainable materials were scarce, sustainable products almost unheard of and they were forced to be creative and inventive to achieve anything at all.

Thanks to them, the availability of sustainable materials has improved hugely. Architects are now far more aware, some are even enthusiastic; builder's merchants, stock admittedly small, ranges of sustainable products and the internet is full of sites with natural and sustainable products, materials and methods.

But the question as to what constitutes a sustainable material can be a difficult one. One definition is a material that has a lower impact on the environment than the non-sustainable alternative.

At one end of the scale there is material from a renewable source, for example, sheep wool insulation or timber from a sustainable forest, that has a very small impact. The impact is not zero as there are issues around harvesting and transport, but in real terms it is the best

4

we can do. Their use has caused no depletion of natural resources, minimal energy has been used in their processing and they have few or zero chemical additives.

At the other end of the scale is material that is just one step up the ladder from the non-sustainable alternative, for example, polypropylene (PP) or polyethylene (PE), which are plastics that are used for pipes or cable insulation as an alternative to PVC. All three use oil as a base material but PP and PE use less energy in the manufacture, have fewer harmful additives and are more easily recycled. The manufacture of PVC can cause the emission of dioxins, PCBs and heavy metals, it is difficult to incinerate as it will emit chlorine and heavy metals and is virtually indestructible in landfill. None of them would achieve a 'good' rating in sustainability terms, one is just a bit better than the other.

In between are a host of materials with more or less sustainable credentials and again it can be difficult to choose between them. The difference between, say, plywood, chipboard and OSB, (oriented strand board) will lie in the glues or bonding agents used and the environmental credentials of the manufacturer. Chipboard and OSB use, primarily, waste wood from other manufacturing processes and plywood uses veneer that is taken from a log. In this case the answer might be that plywood using rainforest veneers is a no-no but there is a trivial ecological difference between chipboard and OSB.

Lime is held up as something of a panacea by the eco-builder in that it is far better than cement in terms of its extraction and processing. Each kg of cement will embody 0.82kg CO_2 compared to just 0.17kg CO_2 in lime. But the reality is that the CO_2 embodied in the cement is far outweighed by the CO_2 embodied in the sand and aggregate that it binds. Making lime concrete, or limecrete, is a particular skill that is scarce in the UK. It may be faster, easier and more environmentally effective to find recycled aggregate and use it with cement to make concrete than to learn how to use lime to make limecrete with virgin aggregate.

There are a few suppliers of recycled aggregate and it is possible to hire crushing machines to turn rubble into re-usable aggregate – if rubble is available in the first place. But even so, recycled aggregate and using lime may both remain impractical. Foamed concrete may be an answer for the floor slab. There are plenty of specialist suppliers around (Google 'foamed concrete' to find some) and the product uses less aggregate, less cement and has better thermal properties than conventional concrete. Concrete is generally a structural component of the building and its strength is usually critical to stability. In sustainability terms, it is best not to use concrete at all, but if it is to be used, it has to be the right concrete.

What will suit in any given project will vary with the circumstances of that project. The material to use for the floor

SUSTAINABLE OPTIONS

4

Element	Preference	Options	Avoid
Foundations	Reclaimed aggregate concrete	Concrete and block	
Ground floor	Suspended timber with reclaimed aggregate blinding	Foamed concrete on reclaimed aggregate sub base	Block and beam
Intermediate floors	FSC timber joists with reclaimed timber boards	FSC timber	Concrete
Walls	FSC timber frame, reclaimed brick	Masonry	Steel frame
Wall cladding	FSC timber, lime render	Masonry	PVC
Windows & doors	Durable timber frames with Low-E double glazing	Aluminium frames	uPVC or PVCu
Roof structure	FSC timber trusses	non-sustainable timber	Steel
Roof covering	Reclaimed slates or tiles, new timber shingles	Concrete roof tiles, clay roof tiles	Copper or Zinc
Finishes	Natural paint on lime plaster	Natural paint on flue-gypsum plaster	Alkyd paint on phospho-gypsum plaster
Floor covering	Linoleum, natural carpets	Ceramic tiles	Vinyl
Gutters, pipes	Galvanised steel	Coated aluminium	PVC, zinc, copper

slab is an example of the decision that will face the builder. A choice between least bad options, or a potentially significant budget overrun.

But it is not always like that. Some of the choices are far clearer. Take flooring. Any rainforest timber is obviously a no-no. Even rainforest timber from a sustainable source is a bit iffy in that doubts exist over the 'sustainability' of the forest and the extraction process usually has a high impact on the local ecology. Reclaimed timber, on the other hand, has excellent credentials and is available from virtually every salvage yard in the country. As it is reclaimed no profit is going to the rainforest timber producers and thereby encouraging the industry, and it has virtually zero embodied energy and CO_2 (that was all taken up in its first use).

Reclaimed timber also has the virtue of being available in a huge variety of sizes, colours

4

and grades. It lends itself well to floorboards, as a decorative finish or to be covered with carpet or lino. Also, the colours and grains that aged timber take on allow more interior design options.

Reclaimed timber is probably not suitable for structural elements, but for internal joinery, flooring and even external fascias and soffits it offers a good alternative.

On the previous page is a list of the main elements of the build with sustainable and less sustainable options and the materials to avoid, if possible. It will come as no surprise that many of the materials in the Avoid list are what would be considered 'traditional'.

The list is not exhaustive and is intended to provide an insight into the types of materials available for each element – and that sustainable options exist for all elements.

SET YOUR OWN TARGETS

It is better to have a building with some sustainable credentials than a building with none. It may be that some elements of the build have to be sacrificed on the altar of practicality or, more usually, finance to achieve a successful project. Personal research will determine which elements can be dealt with sustainably in any given location or project, and making that determination early in the design process will save time, cost and heart-ache.

For the self builder or renovator, education is key. Researching sustainable and recycled materials available in the locality of the project will inform and influence the design of the building. Unless the architect and/or builder are particularly enthusiastic the use of recycled or salvaged materials will be limited to those that the client finds. Local research of architectural salvage and demolition yards can be extremely revealing. From the mundane, recycled roofing slates, to the more esoteric, interesting timber, wrought iron balustrades, landscaping features, antique tiles. It is truly amazing what can be found in good salvage yards. And talk to the guys in the yard and find out what is coming in. You may be able to pre-book a batch of bricks or roof tiles. Knowing what is potentially available will help in the decision-making process and may open up whole new lines of thought.

Recycling material has to be the first objective for a sustainable build, but doubts have been expressed over the transport costs, in terms of CO_2, of using reclaimed material. The following guide, produced by BRE, shows the distance a reclaimed material can be transported by road before it has a greater environmental impact than a new product manufactured locally (within 50 miles).

Returning to the opening statement that sustainability is

about meeting our needs without impacting on the ability of future generations to meet their needs, renovating an existing building is the ultimate in sustainability. It minimises the use of new resources, effectively recycles all the material contained in the building and adds zero transport CO_2. Is it not a shame that there are 1,000s of houses in cities across the country that are being pulled down because they are perceived to have no potential to be

RECLAIMED MILES

Material	Distance (in miles)
Reclaimed tiles	100
Reclaimed slates	300
Reclaimed bricks	250
Reclaimed aggregate	150
Reclaimed timber	1000
Reclaimed steel products	2500
Reclaimed aluminium products	7500

adapted and changed to meet modern needs? Which raises the question, how many modern estates will suffer the same fate?

One of the tenets of sustainability is to design in the potential to be adapted and changed. It is not always easy but, as an example, post and beam construction builds a structure that covers a space with none of the internal walls carrying structural load so that they can be moved at will. The post and beam structure itself can be added to or even reduced and it provides a degree of flexibility not easily found in other construction methods.

The house you are building will last 100 or even 200 years and it is impossible to know what those future generations will need. Designing in adaptability and using materials that can be recycled will at least give them the chance of meeting those needs.

SUSTAINABLE MATERIALS VS SUSTAINABLE DESIGN

Given that the design incorporates decisions around the materials then there is no conflict. However, for the self-builder or renovator, there has to be an expectation that more time, effort and money will be expended in the design phase of the project than would be the case for a conventional build.

A conventional build will require decisions on the size of the property, the construction method (timber-frame or masonry) and style. That will be about it. The architect will specify the materials and the builder will find the cheapest options.

The first area of research for the sustainable builder is to find an architect who understands, and enjoys, sustainability. That in itself may not be easy, but an architect who has no knowledge of sustainability and takes no pleasure from the challenge will

4

make the task impossible.

Next will be to start the process of researching materials, while keeping an idea as to the type of house preferred in the back of the mind. But a pre-determination for a particular material may not be helpful as it will go a long way towards determining the overall design. For example, the client who insists on a green roof will strongly influence everything that goes under it.

In terms of sustainability, the only essential prerequisite is that as many materials as practically possible should be recycled or be from sustainable sources.

The design process then becomes a cycle of finding materials to suit the design and changing the design to suit the materials. Do not be fooled. This will be neither quick nor cheap. What it will produce is a building that gives the owner a strong sense of self-satisfaction; a building that can be boasted about and displayed; and a building that will more than repay its extra design cost in many ways other than financial.

The scope of the sustainable materials made available will be largely a product of the research and effort that the client puts in. Listed below are just a few of the many websites selling sustainable materials.

Some builders' merchants stock sustainable materials, notably Covers on the south coast who

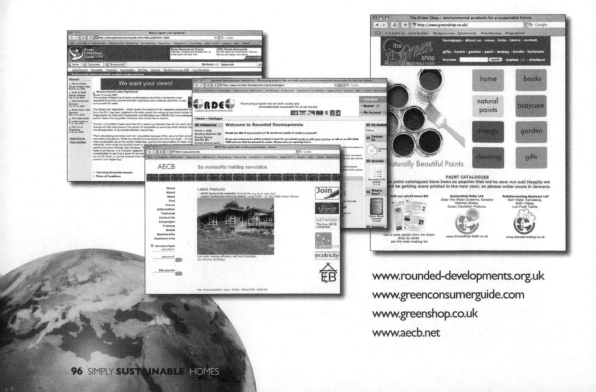

www.rounded-developments.org.uk

www.greenconsumerguide.com

www.greenshop.co.uk

www.aecb.net

4

have Eco-Centres in each of their branches. Most builders' merchants will try to find particular materials if they are asked, so it is well worth finding the material you want and asking the local builders' merchant to supply it. The effect of this is to ease personal supply problems but also to make more sustainable materials available to more people. It may be just a bit of flag waving, but remember the people 10 or 15 years ago who brought us to where we are now.

There is still something of the pioneer spirit involved in sustainable builds and the day may come when all builders' merchants stock a full range of sustainable materials as a matter of course.

TIMBER

Timber will always be a big part of a sustainable build and sustainable timber is fast becoming the accepted norm. Certified sustainable timber is timber that is produced from a forest that is managed to minimise the impact on the ecology and that is grown, harvested and replanted in an environmentally sensitive way. It is far more easily available than was once the case and there are many schemes certifying the sustainability of the timber, including Forestry Stewardship Council (FSC), the Finnish National Certification Scheme, and the UK Woodland Assurance Scheme. The FSC scheme is probably the most widely recognised in the UK, but if in doubt contact Forests Forever for advise.

Another organisation, TRADA, has a very useful website at www.trada.co.uk. It is free, and easy to register and it has a wealth of information on all types and species of timber, including suppliers.

Timber-frame construction has become the de facto standard for a sustainable build. It uses principally a renewable material, minimises production and transport energy and CO_2, and has good structural stability and good thermal performance. Doubts are still being expressed over the longevity of timber-frame, which seems to fly in the face of the evidence that surrounds us. Throughout the UK there are houses 200, 300 or even 400 years old, still standing in good repair and still used on a daily basis. (The author has personal experience of a 600-year-old house, still used as a domestic residence, occupied by descendents of the original builders, and still with all the original roof timbers.) In Japan, there are temples over 2,000 years old, constructed entirely of timber.

The life of a building is determined by the quality of the materials, the quality of the construction and the care in its maintenance. The same factors apply irrespective of the construction method.

4

Durable timber

The durability of timber (its ability to withstand weather) is a factor of three issues: its species, its growth and its processing.

Hardwood species – oak, iroko, sapele, chestnut – are naturally more durable than most softwoods. Some softwood species, for example Douglas fir, are also durable but to a lesser extent. Redwood is a softwood timber with good durability often used in external joinery. Straight grown softwoods, with no knots or shakes that have been slow dried will be far more durable than kiln-dried knotty pine.

Durable timber is useful because it needs little or no treatment to be maintained in good condition, and it lasts. In window and door frames it will outlast PVC with none of the ecological impact. In this country we are lucky to have many examples of old timber buildings using what we would now call durable timber but in those days was just called timber. In the last 60 years the demand for ever-increasing volumes of construction timber has lead to ever-falling quality. We are now accepting timber for structural and joinery purposes that would previously have been rejected as unfit for purpose. That poorer quality has a shorter life, which means that it needs replacing more often, increasing the demand for timber still further.

It needs to be remembered that FSC, or any other certification, says nothing about the timber's quality, only that it comes from a sustainable source. BS5268 provides five classes of durability, plus non durable and perishable. Classes 1 to 3 require no treatment, classes 4 and 5 may need treatment if used externally and non-durable should only be used internally.

Selecting the appropriate species, specifying the class of durability and designing around those issues will minimise the amount of wood needed, eliminate the need for unnecessary toxic treatments and extend the life of the building.

Timber treatments

Forest Forever (www.forestsforever.org.uk) or the Forestry Stewardship Council will also give advice on timber preservation. Again, there are alternatives to the traditional approach of treating every piece of timber with chemical preservatives.

The last 40 years has seen the routine use of some highly-toxic insecticides and fungicides in the timber industry. Much of the application has been to prevent or remedy the premature decay of timber that has come as the result of poor design, using inappropriate timber and inadequate maintenance.

The timber treatment industry has expanded massively and is now a significant sector of the building industry, and, of course, has its own vested interest. We are exhorted daily with TV

4

ads to spray our fences and decking with chemicals to make them last. Remedial treatment of timber is undertaken routinely, at the slightest sign of any timber bio-deterioration, with treatment often a condition of a mortgage offer. Pre-treated timber is routinely specified in buildings where it is difficult to see any justification for it.

Establishing the 'need to treat' underpins British Standards (BS5589 & BS5268 part 5), something that is routinely overlooked. BS5268 Part 5 emphasises good design and the use of appropriate timber: "Where design is unlikely to provide adequate protection, a naturally durable timber or the use of an appropriate preservative treatment should be considered."

The careful selection of timber species, coupled with good design and good building practice, can eliminate the need for chemical treatment. New wood from Durability Classes 4 & 5, non-durable and perishable wood will require treatment when used in exposed situations such as windows, doors, roof tile battens, fascia boards etc. Even then, inorganic boron compounds will be as effective as the chemical alternatives. They are safer and far more environmentally sensitive.

There are a few joinery manufacturers offering naturally-treated durable windows and doors. The Ecoplus System range is one that is pre treated with a glycol borate. Inorganic borate pre-treated roof-tile battens, fascias etc are available in certain parts of the country and The AECB has information on current availability.

For most applications, timber of any durability class does not require treatment for internal carpentry or joinery, although quality remains an issue to ensure it does not warp or bend as it dries in the house.

GREEN ROOFS

Green roofs are, without doubt, one of the more visible signals that what we have here is a sustainable build. And they do have some significant benefits; they absorb heat (from the sun), they absorb CO_2, they absorb a proportion of the water that falls on them (up to 70 percent) and, most importantly, they replace the ecology that the building stands on. London is bringing in regulations to ensure certain types and sizes of building have a green roof, principally for the ecological and heat absorption reasons.

There are two basic types, which can be described as thick and thin. The thick type have a layer of soil of at least 200mm and can support a wide variety of plant, and consequently animal, species. Being thick means that they are heavy and require very substantial support structures. They are normally laid on a reinforced concrete roof. They offer good insulation and better water absorption than the thin types but otherwise are no better. Having a variety

4

ANDREW LEE

Above: the turf roof houses the solar panels, while, in aesthetic terms, it allows the building to fit in with its environment.

This planted sedum roof has two high-performance membranes beneath it that cover 120mm of insulation placed above a vapour barrier.

EVA WARD WWW.WINDHORN.ORG

Maintaining a grass roof can be a problem. He may have been better planting sedum, or similar, that needs no maintenance.

4

of plant species means that some maintenance will be necessary, perhaps even mowing. People have been known to keep goats on the roof for this purpose, but you have to wonder.

Thin green roofs generally have 50mm of soil or other growing medium and are typically planted with sedum. This is a low-growing succulent plant that requires no maintenance in terms of mowing and will put up with short periods of drought. Any growing medium will attract other species and maintenance is likely to remain an issue. The thin green roof has no particular thermal benefits and good insulation will be needed under it, as will a water barrier. They will retain a proportion of the water that falls on then, but gutters and downpipes will still be needed. Although heavy compared to conventional roof coverings they are not so heavy that they cannot be laid on a timber roof structure. They can be used on pitched roofs, but there is not much point as it increases water run-off and they are generally laid to a single, fairly gentle, fall.

The question as to whether a green roof should be an intrinsic part of a sustainable build is open to debate. The clear, incontrovertible, benefit of replacing the ecology that the building stands on can be outweighed by the over-bearing influence that it has on the overall design.

In situations where a green roof suits the design of the building and the topography of the site, especially where the roof can form part of the landscape, it is a great idea. Starting with the premise of a green roof exerts such a strong influence on the structure that it can end up looking out of place and pointless.

WASTE MANAGEMENT

It is an intrinsic part of both the Ecohomes standard and the Code For Sustainable Homes that a waste management plan be prepared and implemented. They are called Site Waste Management Plans (SWMP) and are likely to become compulsory for all building sites in the near future. The reason is that the building industry produces around 72 million tonnes of waste (figure from Chartered Institute of Building) each year and a good proportion of it goes to landfill. 13m tonnes of that is waste material, which is defined by the DTI as waste that was delivered to site, unused and sent to landfill.

A few statistics. The average skip leaving a building site costs about £150 and on average has materials to the value of £1,200 in it. In the UK an average of 13 percent of all materials delivered to site go into the skip without ever being used. The UK produces around 400 million tonnes of waste annually, of which about 72 million tonnes comes from construction

4

sites (if we add demolition sites the figure rises to 109 million tonnes).

The Government website www.netregs.gov.uk gives a lot of information on how to handle and manage waste, but in short it amounts to:

1. Only order enough material and have it delivered 'just in time' to avoid losses during storage.
2. Sort the waste before it hits the skip and reuse everything possible.
3. Sort waste for recycling in separate skips or areas. Sorting metal waste separately may generate income.
4. Avoid 'miscellaneous waste' disposal. Know what is in each skip and where it should be going.

A DTI project carried out by two major housing developers found that careful waste management could reduce the project cost by up to 5 percent.

Another good website is www.wrap.org.uk (Waste & Resources Action Program) who provide advice and guidance on the efficient use and disposal of materials. They also maintain a directory of recycled aggregate suppliers across the UK.

RULES AROUND SUSTAINABLE MATERIALS

1. Find an architect that has knowledge of and enthusiasm for sustainability. Talk to them, visit some houses they have designed and be sure they are what you are looking for.
2. Talk to the architect about the need for other experts – interior designers, lighting designers, contractors, project managers, renewable energy experts. Find those that you need and be sure that both you and the architect can work with them.
3. Have ideas around shape and style, but not fixed ideas.
4. Research materials – what is appealing, what is available, what is local.
5. Be costs conscious – surprises can lead to hasty decisions in the construction phase.
6. Allow design to be an evolutionary process informed by the materials available for the elements that are to be sustainable.

4

7. Firm-up design decisions – decide on construction method.
8. Find a contractor with enthusiasm for sustainability. A good contractor will help with sourcing materials and an unenthusiastic contractor will be a barrier.
9. Specify materials and work-up costs. Projects that come in on time and within budget are the exception rather than the rule.
10. The last budget prepared will be exceeded by at least 20 percent, so make all possible adjustments at the design phase rather than the construction phase.

5 WATER MANAGEMENT

D id you know that the UK has less available water per person than most other European countries and that, technically, London is drier than Istanbul? The whole of the South East has less water available than the Sudan and Syria. This is according to Waterwise, who are a UK NGO responsible for improving water efficiency and are considered to be the leading authority on water use in the UK.

According to Defra, and Waterwise, the average person uses approximately 150 litres of water a day. This has been steadily increasing at a rate of 1 percent per year since 1930. Around 45 litres (30 percent) of this is used for flushing the toilet and only 37 litres is for washing and bathing.

In a paper produced by the DTI entitled 'Strategy for Sustainable Construction: Water Use', it is suggested that a maximum consumption of 120 litres per person per day should be the target for a good sustainability level, and 100 litres in areas where water is scarce. Under the Code for Sustainable Homes there are six code levels and achieving a higher code rating means improving the water efficiency.

Summer 2006 brought one of the worst droughts this country has experienced and summer 2007 one of the worst floods. Floods bring a lot of water, the trouble is that it is not water that can used in the mains supply. In the

WATER CODES

Code Level	Litres per day
1	120
2	120
3	105
4	105
5	80
6	80

2007 flood, large parts of Gloucester and Tewkesbury were under water, but it was weeks after the flood receded before the unhappy residents were able to safely use the mains water supply.

Hose-pipe bans are routine across most of the South of England, in some areas they are permanent. Waterwise maintain that the current levels of water consumption cannot be maintained in the medium to long term (its goal is to significantly reduce consumption by 2010 – which feels more like short term).

In the same way that oil is being recognised as a scarce resource that has to be used with circumspection, water is becoming an equally scarce resource. It is, therefore, necessary for the sustainable builder to give the same consideration to water use as they do to energy use and recycling. And, as we look at energy in and CO_2 out, we need to look at water in and waste out.

WATER IN

There are two issues to consider: the source of the water we take into the house and how efficiently we use it. Looking first at what we take in, there are a couple of options to mains water.

RAINWATER HARVESTING

Rainwater harvesting is the most obvious way of countering our dependence on mains water and making better, and cheaper, use of the water that is available. It is a practice that has been followed for thousands of years and archaeologists have found evidence of its use in the Negev desert from 4000 years ago, and in Ancient Roman villas.

Calculating how much water is potentially available is relatively easy, as we have a good idea as to average rainfall. The calculation is:

Roof area x annual rainfall x run-off coefficient x filter coefficient

The roof area is the horizontal area covered by the roof in m^2 (usually slightly larger than the foot print). The annual rainfall varies across the country but the figure of 900mm is a good average. The run-off coefficient relates to the type of roof covering and amount of water that will be held on the roof, lost to wind and evaporation. The filter coefficient relates to the harvesting system itself, but again in both cases the figures given are good averages.

5

So for our 200m² house the footprint will be 100m² and the roof area 110m².
This gives: 110 × 900 × 0.75 × 0.9 = 66,825 litres pa.

By way of comparison, a house with four people in occupation will use, at a rate of 150 litres per person per day, 219,000 litres per year. At a rate of 80 litres per day (the Code for Sustainable Homes and Waterwise targets), it would be 116,800 litres per year.

There are a number of different kinds of systems, but essentially they fall into above ground or below ground. Typically domestic systems have an underground tank and filter, and a submersible pump.

Garden systems use a filter attached to the guttering downpipes and filter the water into a free-standing above-ground tank.

Header tank systems include a mains water supply inlet so that rainwater will fill the tank when it's available. When there is no supply from the pump, the mains water inlet will open. This function, of providing mains water back up, is usually an optional extra with all domestic systems.

Basic components

Tank – Either above ground or below ground, the tank will be sized to the roof area (the potential collection). Typical domestic sizes are 2,500 litres to 10,000 litres. They are typically plastic – polyethylene – but sometimes concrete. Some manufacturers offer recycled polyethylene, notably Wisy tanks. The design and installation of the tank is important as an empty tank will tend to 'float' in a high water table and tanks have been known to break through the surface.

Filters – Typically there are up to four filters in a domestic system. An initial filter sifts out the larger items of debris, leaves etc, followed by the calming inlet filter which ensures that when the water enters the base of the tank it doesn't disturb any silt on the bottom. Next is the overflow filter positioned near the top of the tank that skims the surface for any lighter particles. Finally, there is the pump inlet floating filter, just beneath the surface of the water.

Harvested rainwater is normally used for 'grey water' applications – flushing the toilet, washing machines, cleaning the car – as the water is not clean enough to be used as drinking water (and there generally is not enough of it). Cleaning the water to potable standards can be done and just needs two extra filters: a mechanical filter – typically stainless steel or glass granules – which filters particles down to five microns, and an ultra-violet light filter which kills bacteria. A potable water filter system will add

5

around £650 to £900 to the price of the system.

Pumps – either a submersible or suction pump is needed to convey the water from the tank to the house. The submersible pumps are mounted in the tank and have a floating inlet that draws water from 200mm below the surface of the water to avoid picking up any floating debris. Being in the tank they are practically silent in operation but more tricky to get at for servicing or maintenance. Suction pumps are mounted above the tank or in the house. They are, therefore, slightly more noisy and easier to maintain, but prone to sucking in air.

Rainwater collection system – essentially pipework from the guttering downpipes, through the initial filter, to the tank. Usually these are supplied as part of the overall system.

Rainwater harvesting systems are now widely available, and becoming increasingly popular. A typical domestic system will currently cost between £2,500 and £4,500. The price is falling as popularity increases and it is easy to see that they will become a standard feature of new builds in the not too distant future.

Below is a list of companies able to supply individual components or complete systems

Stormsaver Ltd

Ecovision Systems Ltd

EcoFirst Ltd

Source Control Systems Ltd

Hydro International

Rainwater Harvesting Systems Ltd.

BOREHOLES

These are created, essentially, by drilling a 150mm to 200mm diameter hole in the ground deep enough to hit the water table (as it will vary from winter to summer), inserting a pipe and pumping out water – similar to an artesian well. A number of water authorities take some or all of their water from aquifers or the water table so a borehole may not actually reduce the drain on the natural resource. What it does do is significantly reduce the energy and infrastructure needed to convey the water from the aquifer to the house.

The practicality, depth and cost of a borehole will be entirely dependent on the location. The aquifer or water table may be 10m below ground level or 100m and this obviously has a direct impact on the potential cost and the suitability. As a guide, a borehole capped with a manhole with a suitable pump installed will cost not less than £2,500 and could get over

5

£20,000 – dependent entirely on location.

The big advantage of a borehole is that it will meet 100 percent of the water needs of the house. But that is no reason to be profligate with the resource.

As with rainwater, borehole water is technically not clean enough to drink and a fine particle filter and UV disinfection will be needed, which will cost £650 to £900. What you get is water without added fluoride, chlorine or aluminium sulphate, the chemicals that water companies insist we need – and about which the home owner must make their own decision.

WATER USE

Whatever the scarcity or otherwise of water, it is difficult to deny it is becoming an increasingly expensive resource. In the North of England, the average un-metered bill is around £229 while across southern England the average bill is £324. In the west of England the average un-metered customer pays £650 per year.

If we assume that a rainwater harvesting system has a life of 20 years, the capital cost of an installed system of £4,500 looks fairly cheap at £225 per year. That cost is fixed for 20 years, unlike water charges that have been given approval to rise by 18 percent over the next five years.

An issue to bear in mind is that it is becoming mandatory in an increasing number of water utility areas to install water meters in all new housing, or where there is any change to the existing supply. Notionally this is so that water companies can reduce the amount they charge by only charging for what is actually consumed. If that policy is fully implemented it will result in a substantial reduction in water company profits – a trend that is not immediately recognisable in any utility company. What it does do is make us aware of the amount of water we actually consume. That is at least a first step on the way to reducing our consumption.

However, the water gets to the house, and whatever its source, it needs to be used efficiently – or to put it another way, sparingly – and there is a plethora of equipment available to help. Here we deal with each of the four main means of water use in turn.

MACHINES

Taken together, dishwashers and washing machines account for about 28 percent of the domestic water consumption. The Waterwise website at waterwise.org.uk/reducing_water_ wastage_in_the_uk/house_and_garden ranks the most water efficient machines currently available on the UK market.

TAPS

There are a number of different types of taps and fittings for taps that can save water, for example, proximity detection taps that only operate when a hand is near (and because you don't need to touch the tap they are said to be more hygienic). There are aerated taps that use less water than they appear to, and there are taps that have two pressure settings, a low pressure in the first position and a higher pressure in the second. There are also products that can be fitted to existing taps to make them more economic, for example, water-reducing valves, which can be fitted to all appliances to reduce the flow. Also bear in mind the costs incurred from leaking and dripping taps – a dripping tap can waste enough water in a day to run a shower for five minutes.

Flow restrictor valves These can be fitted to all taps and limit the flow rate to the required minimum. They are DIY to fit and apparently will save up to 70 percent of the water used, at a cost of as little as £3.79.

Spray taps The basic spray taps are widely available and are very reasonably priced, for example, a pair of standard bathroom taps can cost as little as £30. By spraying water they achieve a larger 'wetted area' with a lower flow rate.

Push taps These can be added to existing taps by replacing the top of the tap with a push tap conversion. Cost is around £24 per unit and they save water by shutting-off the flow after a few seconds.

Sensor taps The main selling point of these products, in addition to the water saving benefits of course, seems to be that it is the most hygienic tap on the market. Mains or battery operated will cost around £400 for a pair.

Bear in mind that reduced-flow taps may not be appropriate for main kitchen and bath taps as they simply increase the time needed to fill the sink or bath – consider using a variable flow-rate tap in this case instead.

TOILETS

The toilet is the single largest user of water in the home – 30 percent to 35 percent of

5

total consumption. Reducing the amount of water used can be achieved by simply putting a brick in the cistern.

For those wishing to be a little more discerning they could try a Hippo Bag. A pack of 10 bags will cost £10 from Ecoptopia, and by simply inserting them into your cistern (of 9 litres capacity) you could save between 2.5 and 3.5 litres of water per flush. Some water authorities give them out for free, one of which is Welsh Water.

For the even more discerning is the Interflush. It is a kit that fits onto the siphon and connects to the front mounted flush handle. It works by ensuring the toilet only flushes when the handle is held down. Once the handle is released the flush stops. It could save up to 30 litres of water per person per day and will only cost around £20.

Delayed action inlet valves Although toilets are rated with 9, 7 or 6-litre cisterns, they actually use water more than this. As soon as the cistern is flushed it starts refilling, and goes on trying to refill the cistern until there is insufficient water to maintain the siphon and the flush stops. That extra water is more than was needed and is lost. A valve is available that remains shut when the flush has started and only opens to refill the cistern once the flushed water has drained away.

Dual-flush and low-flush toilets These cut household water use by up to 20 percent (so says the Environment Agency) and save more than half the water used to flush the toilet. The standard flow for a dual-flush cistern is two and four litres per flush. Ultra-low flush toilets will use about a third less water than a standard cistern – two to three litres per flush. In a study carried out at St Leonards Primary School in Hastings, there was a saving of nearly 40 percent in the water used to flush the toilets (kent.gov.uk).

Dry toilets For the really committed among us, there is the dry toilet. They work by providing an enclosed environment to collect the waste and provide aerobic decomposition. They can be installed in the home just like normal toilets and use little or no water. They are not connected to the sewerage system so that you can recycle your own waste for use in the garden (but hopefully this is not compulsory!). They are expensive, comparatively speaking, and will cost around £1000 installed.

SHOWERS

Having a shower rather than a bath is a good step towards saving water. A five-minute shower uses 35 litres while a bath can use around 80 litres. Below are a few examples of the types of shower available, although they are all similar in principal to the water-saving taps on the market.

As with taps, one way of saving water in shower-heads is by reducing the flow. A typical flow will be 15 to 20 litres per minute and these restricted flow heads cut this to around 8 litres per minute. They are relatively cheap at around £25 and can be used with power-showers and shower pumps.

Some shower heads accelerate the water flow, energising and oxygenating it. This increases the pressure of the shower and gives the impression that more water is being providing than there actually is.

There are also electronic showers on the market, like the sensor taps, that only operate when movement is detected. They have an in-built flow regulator at six litres per minute, although it can be deactivated to give 15 l/m. It is available as a mains operated device as well as battery operated, and retails at around £750.

Generally, water saving showers seem to have exactly the same effect on water savings as taps, but with generally less customer satisfaction, probably for obvious reasons.

GREY WATER RECYCLING

Grey water is water that has been used specifically for washing, from laundry, dishwashers, baths, showers and hand washing, which could be reused for toilet flushing or watering the garden. The three grades of water are clean (or potable), grey and black. Black is that from toilets, or with other pollutants that need a high level of treatment to be reusable, potable is clean water than needs no treatment, and grey water is somewhere between. It needs a bit of treatment, but not too much.

A grey water system does not rely on any specific kind of building or level of rainfall and can therefore be used in any type of household. The amount of grey water available is largely dependent on whether baths and showers are used, but in all cases it makes a significant contribution to the overall water consumption.

5

The price of a grey water recycling system varies from £20 (for a siphon pump) to £2,500, compared to £2,500 to £4,500 for rainwater harvesting, and saves nearly as much water. The average rainwater harvesting system will produce between 30 percent and 50 percent of the overall consumption, compared to 20 percent to 40 percent for grey water. They also tend to be a lot easier to install as they do not always require a large-capacity tank buried in the garden, although some of the larger, more complex systems do.

The Water Green pump

At the lower end of the market, this is basically a siphon for emptying the bath. It is merely a tube with a built-in siphon primer bulb and a standard hosepipe fitting. One end of the tube is placed into the bath or sink that is to be emptied and the other end is fed through the window and connected to a hosepipe. The siphon primer pump is then squeezed a few times and the water is drawn up through the pipe. Providing that the 'water out end' of the pipe is below the height of the bottom of the bath, the water will continue to be sucked out.

This is most suitable if the grey water is for immediate reuse, for example, garden watering. The water should not to be used on any edible crops and if it is to be stored for use later on then it should be disinfected.

The Water Green Pump is available at £19.99.

STORAGE TANK

CLEANING TANK

The Ecoplay greywater management system re-cycles bath and shower water and uses it to flush toilets.

Ecoplay System

This may be considered a more typical and more complete system in that it automatically collects grey water and prepares it specifically for toilet flushing. As such it replaces the need for clean water for flushing and, therefore, directly saves 30 percent of the overall consumption.

The system comprises a cleaning tank, where the water is collected and cleaned, a storage tank, with a capacity of 100 litres, and a control unit. This has a built-in computer that monitors the quality of the

5

stored water, how long the water is stored for, how often the toilet is flushed and how often water is taken from baths and showers. Water that is stored too long is drained off to the sewerage system. It also ensures that water is immediately drained off to prevent stagnation if there is a power failure.

There are a number of systems like this that are designed specifically for recycling water solely for flushing the toilet. Costs tend to be in the £900 to £1000 bracket.

The AquaCycle 900

This type of system is further up the scale again, possibly at the top. It is a biomechanical process that takes water from bath, shower, washing machine, dishwasher and treats it for use to flush toilets, re-use in the washing machine or in the garden for irrigation or washing the car. It can treat up to 600 litres of water per day, which is equivalent to the average daily consumption for a four-person household.

The system comprises three tanks in which the water is filtered, treated and UV disinfected so that the outflow water is as close to being potable as can be without actually being potable.

The system can also accept harvested rainwater, in an optional extra tank, and the price is close to a rainwater harvesting system.

The reason that grey water is not used in baths and showers is the same as why it is not used as drinking water. In a bath or shower there is the potential for water to get in the bather's mouth, together with any pollutants that may lurk in the grey water after it has been

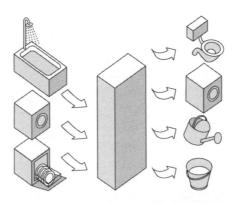

The AquaCycle® 900 cleans and stores water from the shower, bath, washing machine allowing you to use it for your toilet, garden, laundry or domestic cleaning.

5

filtered. Some of the systems clean the water so well that it is indistinguishable from drinking water, but as responsibility for the cleaning rests with the user, the manufacturer is, wisely, not prepared to advertise it as drinking quality water.

WATER OUT

There are four ways of dealing with the waste water leaving the building: direct it to the main sewer, direct it to a septic tank, use a micro treatment plant (a bio-digester) or construct a reed bed.

In terms of sustainability, there is very little to choose between the first three options. With the exception of reed beds the process is largely the same and it is a matter of where the treatment takes place rather than improving the treatment. The processes all leave a highly polluting sludge and the question is always ultimately how to dispose of it.

Only reed beds provide a sustainable solution in that they take no energy, are self-sustaining, produce a useful by-product – reeds – and have no resulting sludge. The outflow water can be from grey to very pale grey, depending on the extent of the reed bed. At the lowest level, it produces water that is clean enough to maintain a healthy ecology in a pond or stream.

REED BEDS

The principles of a reed bed are fairly simple. The common reed (Phragmites Australis) has the ability to transfer oxygen from its leaves, down the stem and out via the root system. As a result of this oxygenation, a high population of micro organisms flourish in the root system. Essentially, the reeds provide a surface on which other organisms can grow and proliferate. These organisms (fungi, algae, mosses and aquatic invertebrates) have the ability to remove contaminant from the incoming water. For example, certain species of fungi have the ability to remove a range of synthetic chemicals including pesticides and chlorinated hydrocarbons. Reed beds can be constructed to remove specific contaminants either biologically or by chemical or physical filtration, sedimentation and absorption.

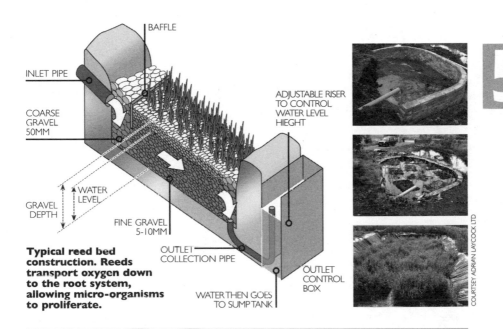

BAFFLE

INLET PIPE

COARSE
GRAVEL
50MM

ADJUSTABLE RISER
TO CONTROL
WATER LEVEL
HIEGHT

WATER
LEVEL

GRAVEL
DEPTH

FINE GRAVEL
5-10MM

OUTLET
COLLECTION PIPE

OUTLET
CONTROL
BOX

WATER THEN GOES
TO SUMP TANK

COURTESY ADRIAN LAYCOCK LTD

Typical reed bed construction. Reeds transport oxygen down to the root system, allowing micro-organisms to proliferate.

Construction

Reed beds normally have an impermeable liner (usually high-density polyethylene) to ensure that the effluent material is contained until it has been fully treated. On this will be a gravel bed, which can be made up of different grades of gravel or sand. The type of gravel used will depend on the intended use of the bed and the quality of material entering it. For example, iron rich sands or a soil and seashell mixture are used specifically to remove phosphorous. Most reed beds are constructed to have a subsurface flow and for these the gravel layer is constructed with a coarser layer at the bottom with a lighter support material on top.

Flow System

There are two kinds of reed bed, a horizontal or vertical-flow bed. Horizontal-flow systems are the most popular type for domestic purposes and systems usually have a gradient of 1 in 100, and a depth of 0.6m to 0.7m. The flow of waste water into a horizontal bed is a continuous one, with a designated inlet and outlet.

Vertical-flow systems are similar to horizontal beds in their materials. The principal difference is that the reed bed is flooded and the waste water is allowed to drain down through the system and then out again. Once it is dry, oxygen will refill the voids left within the system, replenishing the supply. In some vertical-flow systems, perforated pipes are added to increase oxygen levels still further.

5

Beds can be set up separately or with interconnecting beds that may run in series or in parallel. In each of these cases it is wise to rotate the beds to ensure that those receiving untreated waste water are swapped for those receiving partially treated waste water. This will ensure that beds aren't exhausted.

A good installer – YES Reed Beds (yes-reedbeds.co.uk) is one – will design and construct the right bed, sort out all the Environment Agency paperwork and re-visit the bed after construction to ensure it is working properly.

The price of a reed bed will depend on size. A normal domestic size bed will be 4m² to 6m² and cost in the order of £1,500 to £2,000.

PERMEABLE SURFACE TREATMENTS

Limiting surface water run-off, principally by using permeable treatments, form an integral part of both Ecohomes and the Code for Sustainable Homes. The motivation to take on the 10 percent to 15 percent increase in cost over standard surface treatments is not easy to grasp. The direct effect of efficient energy use is a reduction in running costs. A supplementary effect is a reduction in CO_2 emissions, which has little effect on the individual emitting the CO_2, but a potentially massive effect if everyone does it. Limiting surface water run off follows the same argument but without the reduction in running costs.

Typically gentle rain produces 90 litres of water per hour on any one driveway, while a summer storm might produce 630 litres. It is estimated (by Acheson-Glover) that rainfall will increase in volume by up to 40 percent in the next 50 years, and that the incidence of summer storms will also increase. Add to that the increasing rate of building and, to put it simply, the existing system of sewers cannot be extended or enlarged quickly enough to cope.

Surface water run-off hitting the sewer system increases the amount of pollutants carried into the watercourse, reduces the amount of water recharging aquifers and increases the risk of flash-flooding. Using a permeable treatment could reduce the amount of water entering a sewer by up to 80 percent.

The simple answers for homes and gardens, would be mulches. These are best used in infrequently used areas, but barks and pebbles would probably be the cheapest and most effective solutions, closely followed by crushed rocks and gravel. For something a little more sturdy consider the following.

PERMEABLE CONCRETE AND ASPHALT

This is essentially the same as standard concrete or asphalt, but made with a single-size aggregate. The effect of this is to leave gaps between each piece of aggregate, through which water can penetrate.

As with all permeable surface treatments, it requires special treatment to the sub-strata to maintain stability and to allow the water to drain into the soil, and eventually find the water table.

The product itself is no more difficult to find than standard concrete or asphalt but may be a little more expensive. Constructing a suitable substrate takes more time and thought but also should not be too much more expensive.

This option works in terms of water run-off, but it is still a hard surface that does nothing for the ecology. Following, are a couple of examples of products that retain, if not enhance, the ecology.

GRASS PAVERS

The first system, and my favourite, is grass paving. Below are illustration of the Netpave system, a construction illustration and an installed area.

Netpave 50 – the Netpave system is a grid, consisting of connecting lugs and slots. It is flexible and can therefore be laid over uneven surfaces and gradients. It is in-filled with soil and grass (or for drives and parking areas, gravel) and as the cellular structure is open, it allows development of a strong root system and free drainage. Suitable for

Grass pavers require little preparatory work, and no more than a non-permeable surface.

5

permanent car parks, drives and pathways.

Netpave 25 – This is a new product and differs from Netpave 50 in that it is laid over existing grass rather than having grass planted into it. Again it is extremely flexible and can become almost invisible as grass grows around it. It can also be laid temporarily if needed, unlike Netpave 50, although it has been designed for permanent use.

Grasscrete – essentially exactly the same as Netpave (different manufacturer), but is a cellular reinforced concrete system. It is load bearing up to 40 tonnes gross vehicle weight.

Each of these items are easily installed with no pegging required. They are resistant to deformation and rutting and, according to the manufacturers, aesthetically pleasing.

PERMEABLE PAVEMENTS

Essentially these are block paved surfaces for patios and the like, with wide joints filled with fine aggregate. This is then laid on a free-draining base. As the water passes through the base course it is filtered (studies from Coventry University have indicated that up to 97 percent of hydrocarbons are filtered out in this process).

Permeable pavements are suitable for all the usual residential applications, including drives, car parking, patios and footpaths. They have the same attributes as the slabs or blocks they are constructed with.

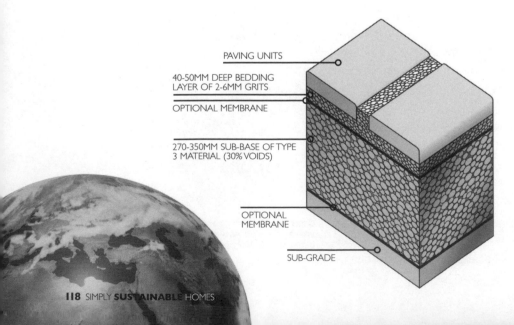

PAVING UNITS

40-50MM DEEP BEDDING
LAYER OF 2-6MM GRITS

OPTIONAL MEMBRANE

270-350MM SUB-BASE OF TYPE
3 MATERIAL (30% VOIDS)

OPTIONAL
MEMBRANE

SUB-GRADE

The type of system that you will use will depend on topography and the quality of the soil. An installer should be able to help you determine which is suitable for your home. You will need to ascertain what kind of soil you have and the rainfall levels in your area. This will determine the sub-base thickness needed to support the system on top.

This is the usual structure of a block-paved area. Directly under the paving units will be a bedding layer, typically sharp sand or 6mm grit. For extra help removing pollutants a geo-membrane can be added under the bedding material. It will catch any hydrocarbons as well as any organic material, which can then be allowed to decompose. This is usually only installed in car-parking areas. If there is a higher risk of pollutants then another impermeable membrane can be added between the sub base and the sub grade to trap them.

The overall efficiency of the system will diminish over time as the voids have a tendency to become clogged up with salts, mud and silts, but this can be solved with jet washing.

As with all things, especially new things, if you are going to do it, it is best to do it right. The Association of Block Paving Contractors have been set up to promote and maintain the highest standard of practice, develop installation techniques and increase the pool of competent installers. So it seems wise to seek the assistance of an approved installer. A comprehensive list can be found on www.interlay.org.uk.

From the above, it can be seen that the real benefit of permeable surface treatments is for the local ecology. Hard surfaces do nothing to help or encourage flora and fauna; they prevent water reaching underground aquifers and reflect heat. They also help to increase the pollution reaching rivers and watercourses. How important that is to the individual builder is a matter for that individual. It is clearly important to the country at large.

CONCLUSION

At this moment, we don't know how much water we need to save. Waterwise suggest 20 percent, but it is difficult to see the science behind this as we still do not know what the true effects of global warming will be. James Lovelock, the man who developed the Gaia principle and first brought global warming to our attention in the 1970s, was asked what we should expect from global warming. His answer was: 'Surprises'. Cool, wet summers; warm, wet winters; hot, dry summers, they all seem to be on the cards and all come as a surprise, so maybe he is right.

What we know is that the existing water and sewage infrastructure needs around £46 billion spending on it to meet the demand expected between now and 2050. When have our Governments ever got the expected demand right?

6 100% SUSTAINABLE

Do you have the pioneering spirit? You will need to if you want to try and achieve a truly sustainable home.

In terms of reaching 100 percent sustainability, the big things – floors, walls, roof – are fairly easy to deal with. Straw bale, sustainable timber, reclaimed roof slates are all relatively easy to source and deal with. The devil lies in the detail. Walls need finishing and even lime plaster is processed and has embodied energy and CO_2. Kitchen fittings can be made from reclaimed timber, but recycled cupboard door hinges are hard to find. Electric cable can contain a proportion of recycled copper, but the insulation tends to be virgin PVC.

In building a sustainable home we are trying to achieve two things:

1. Reduce the amount of irreplaceable natural resources used in the building.
2. Reduce the carbon footprint of the building, both embodied carbon and the carbon emitted in running.

To achieve 100 percent sustainability, we would need to reduce both those to zero.

The Government requires that by 2016 (or 2012 in Wales) ALL new homes are 'Carbon Zero'. As has been discussed in the Materials section, a conventionally built house will embody some 44 tonnes of CO_2 in its materials. A sustainably built house, using modern methods and sustainable materials will maybe halve the embodied CO_2. So the mantra of 'towards zero carbon' is a bit misleading to say the least. Even the poor tribes people of Ethiopia emit 0.1 tonnes of CO_2 per person, and no one is suggesting that Europeans, Americans, Australians, et al, should live like Ethiopians. Rather that Ethiopians should be helped to achieve the same standards the rest of the world enjoys.

Calculating the carbon footprint of a building remains a nutty problem. What to include in the calculation is still a matter of debate. The question goes: 'Do we include the energy used to cook the breakfast for the driver of the lorry that delivered the sheep

6

wool insulation?' Or to put it another way, where do you stop?

The answer generally is that footprint means what footprint says. Transporting materials has to be a factor and local sourcing is a fundamental tenet of sustainability. But, as has been shown, renewable and reclaimed materials can travel a long way before they take up as much carbon as locally-produced virgin material.

Aiming at 100 percent sustainability and zero carbon emissions is laudable, so long as it is recognised that it is utopia – an unachievable ideal.

LOW-ENERGY HOMES

BEDZED
www.peabody.org.uk/bedZED

The BedZED concept was to create a net 'zero fossil energy development' of 82 residential homes: variously flats, apartments and houses. The aim was to construct a development that would produce at least as much energy from renewable sources as it consumes. The project also has commercial buildings, an exhibition centre and a children's nursery, in effect a complete working community.

Buildings use concrete and masonry to give thermal mass that stores heat during warm conditions and releases it at cooler times; they do not adopt the light-tight principles being advocated today. In addition, all buildings have a minimum of 300mm insulation. It is interesting to note that the project started in 2001 when 300mm of insulation was considered a lot. At that time, the Building Regs called for just 100mm of loft insulation. Today Building Regs call for 270mm minimum loft insulation and Passiv Haus and similar standards will use up to 500mm.

Houses are arranged in south-facing terraces to maximise solar heat gain and each terrace is backed by north-facing offices, where minimal solar gain reduces the tendency to overheat.

Emphasis was given to natural, recycled or

The BedZED concept was to create a net 'zero fossil energy development'

6

reclaimed materials and sourced, where possible, within a 35-mile radius of the site. Taken together these reduced the embodied energy and CO_2 in the buildings.

The buildings were designed to be heated principally by solar gain and 'casual heat gains' – cooking, occupants, and the like. The design also incorporated passive natural ventilation which together significantly reduced the need for space heating.

BedZED receives electrical power from a small-scale combined heat and power plant (CHP), which also provides hot water and supplements the space heating. The CHP plant is fuelled by woodchip and has experienced some problems in operation. One of which was educating the residents in how the houses operated. The immediate effect of this lack of education was that more heat was needed than had been planned for. These problems have been largely ironed out and the plant is expected to be fully operational in 2007.

BedZED was a pioneering project that required the co-operation and involvement of the residents to succeed. The first residents moved in during March 2002 and many lessons were learnt and many modifications to the design made as a result of resident's experience.

STEWART MILNE SIGMA HOMES

www.stewartmilne.com

The Code for Sustainable Homes gives a star rating to new homes; the maximum rating is six stars, which is a building with zero carbon emissions. The house built by Stewart Milne Group has achieved a five-star rating which represents a 100 percent improvement on Part L Building Regulations, a 30 percent reduction in water use and zero CO_2 emissions from heating, hot water, ventilation and lighting. It uses timber-frame construction, light and tight, solar thermal panels, PV panels and wind turbines.

It is said to be a commercially viable product for the urban housing developer and to have a host of environment-friendly features, including grey-water recycling and rainwater harvesting.

HANSON ECO-HOUSE

This is a masonry-built, three-bedroom house, constructed from pre-fabricated brick panels. It gained a four-star rating and has high levels of insulation, natural ventilation and PV panels. This means that it is 44 percent better than Part L Building Regs and uses 12 percent less water. Some way off zero carbon but still acclaimed as a Low-Energy

6

House. Pre-fabricating the brick panels is said to reduce waste by up to 20 percent, but the embodied energy and CO_2 is still high compared to timber-frame.

KINGSPAN LIGHTHOUSE

Said to be the most advanced house design ever produced for mainstream construction. It is the only design currently available that achieves a six-star rating on the Code for Sustainable Homes, which means that it has net zero carbon emissions, uses 33 percent less water than a conventional house and uses A-rated materials from the Green Guide for Housing Specification.

The building is a 93m², two-and-a-half storey, two-bedroom house and is constructed using Kingspan Off-Site's TEK Building System. This gives an overall U-value of 0.11W/m²K and airtightness of less than 1.0m²/hr/m², which reduces heat loss by around two-thirds compared to a conventional house.

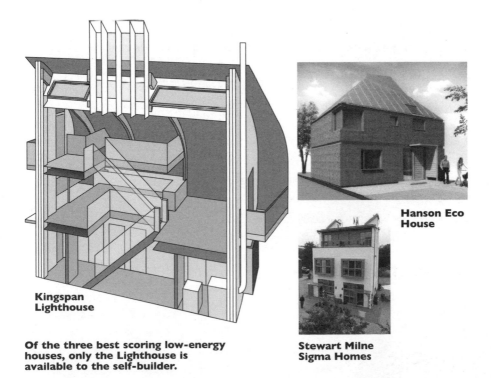

Kingspan Lighthouse

Of the three best scoring low-energy houses, only the Lighthouse is available to the self-builder.

Hanson Eco House

Stewart Milne Sigma Homes

6

One of the more interesting features is a biomass boiler and a waste separation system, which enables combustible waste to be used locally in the central heat and power plant. The building also incorporates integrated photovoltaic, solar-thermal array, mechanical ventilation with heat recovery and a roof-mounted wind catcher, which provides passive cooling and ventilation.

Conclusions on Low-Energy Housing

All these houses (except BedZED) can be seen at the BRE centre in Watford on their Innovation Park, Offsite 2007 display.

The major players in the housing industry, or at least those with something to prove, are all putting forward a 'product' variously labelled as Low-Energy, Zero Carbon or Sustainable. Whether they actually achieve what they say is a moot point, but really not too relevant. The fact that they are investing small fortunes in developing these products and systems indicates two things:

1. They believe that the market is, or will be, keen to buy their products.
2. Significantly reducing the energy used in the home and improving a building's sustainability is achievable.

Whatever else these projects and products have done, they have moved the game on. Some of the ideas coming out of these projects are good and innovative, some seem plain daft. But it doesn't matter. Kingspan insulation can never be considered a sustainable product, but the fact that the company is prepared to invest millions in developing more sustainable building systems is important and useful. It stimulates and motivates the market by putting otherwise obscure products in the mainstream. It increases awareness of sustainability and reducing energy consumption in those most difficult to reach – the local small builder – and makes life easier for the self builder or renovator aspiring to sustainability.

SOLAR-POWERED HOUSING

The question is can solar power alone provide enough energy to power a house? The answer is, well, almost.

Solar power for electricity production is not a problem. Photovoltaic systems are well proven technology and it is just a

6

matter of size and considerable cost.

Solar power for space and water heating is a different matter. In addition to a south-facing roof, a south-facing conservatory and a glazed roof to collect passive solar heat, floors and walls designed with masonry mass to store heat and release it when the sun is not shining will also be required. In addition, of course, a substantial solar-thermal system is required to heat water.

More time and money will need to be spent on the design to ensure excellent insulation and good ventilation to give the movement of warmed air to minimise the heat load of the building. Mechanical heat recovery will also be needed to capture casual heat gains (from cooking, lighting, showers, etc) as will high-performance double, or even triple glazing. Construction costs should be similar to a traditional house of the same size with money going to design and insulation rather than central heating.

Even then, a 'top-up' of solar energy with an immersion heater in the hot water tank and maybe a log-burning stove is likely to be necessary. On clear frosty days, there's enough sun to generate the heat needed, but on cloudy winter's days there probably won't be.

In conclusion, solar heating works, and it has been done, most notably in Cornwall. But it probably does not work as well in Orkney. The UK can provide plenty of free energy – in Cornwall it may be solar and in Orkney probably wind – and the key is designing a house to take advantage of what is available. Done properly, it will work, but the investment will be in design and equipment rather than running costs.

SUSTAINABLE CONSTRUCTION HOMES

The number of people actually attempting to build with cheap, natural materials like mud, hemp and straw is very small – until the end of 2006 only two mortgages had been given by the Ecological Building Society for straw-bale homes. But there are people alive today who were born and raised in cob houses. It must also be considered that although the raw material is cheap, the cost of the building will not be much less than a conventional build, if at all. These materials and methods only apply to the walls and are off-setting the cost of timber-frame or masonry. The costs involved in the rest of the property remain the same and the time taken to build a straw-bale or cob wall will probably absorb all the cost saving in materials, unless there is lots of free labour to hand.

Although many people start out thinking that it is a cheap building method, it is not principally about cost saving. It is about sustainability, a tiny embodied carbon footprint and lifestyle. It is labour intensive, it means learning new, rare skills, it requires determination to get

6

it past the regulators, it needs careful thought and even more careful planning. But the sense of satisfaction from completing a home of this sort can only be wondered at. It is something you do because you want to and when you're finished it is guaranteed to make you smile.

COB HOUSES

Cob is an old word for a mud wall, and Devon and the south west probably have more cob than anywhere else in Britain, cob being Devon and Cornwall's traditional construction material from the fourteenth century. There are still cob houses standing in the West Country that were built over 400 years ago. In 1998, Bob Bennett, a specialist in single skin wall construction, together with a small team of enthusiasts, built a single-storey cob house in a day, in a clearing in the New Forest. The object was to prove a piece of folklore that in medieval times, if a peasant without rights could build a house on common land between sunrise and sunset, he could claim the building for his own.

Cob is a mixture of straw (around 3 percent by dry weight), and sometimes dung, added to a clay sub soil. In some parts of the country, notably Hampshire, chalk is also added. The straw and dung (although some sources maintain that the dung element is a myth) are added to reduce cracking problems in the clay during drying. Traditionally cattle would be used to tread the mixture, so the addition of dung would seem to be inevitable. Today, a JCB or similar is used to mix the straw and clay, and dung is optional. As about 70 percent of the earth's land mass is clay, this seems like quite a good material in terms of sustainability.

The cob is mixed with water to a 'just workable' consistency and the walls built up in layers, with each layer being rammed and given time to dry before the next one is added. Shuttering can be used to aid stability during construction and the wall finished with a 'bag rub' – literally rubbing with a hessian sack to give a textured finish. This construction method brings one of the great advantages of cob. It can take on a much wider variety of lateral shapes. Sweeping curves and round corners are no more difficult than straight lines and can lead to interesting design ideas.

A good-quality cob can survive quite well without rendering, but normally it is coated with a lime render, followed by a lime wash. These coatings have the important property of being porous, or 'breathable', so that any moisture that gets into the cob, via penetrating rain or rising damp, can evaporate out through the render. Moisture is the death of cob (for obvious reasons) and good cob walls are said to have 'a good hat and a good set of boots'. The good hat is the roof covering, which is traditionally thatch and

6

usually has widely overhanging eaves to ensure there is no rain water penetration to the top of the wall. The good boots are a stone or masonry foundation plinth. The plinth will usually be up to 600mm above ground level, to minimise splashing from rainwater hitting the ground, and will have to incorporate a damp-proof course (DPC) to comply with current building regulations (although strictly it is not necessary as cob walls work by allowing any moisture penetration to drain away). Often draining foundations are used, which are a cavity stone or block wall with a loose stone infill to allow moisture in the cob to drain away.

A typical cob house with thatch roof. A modern version would be almost indistinguishable to this old example.

Built properly, cob walls are extremely durable. Most modern coatings, such as cement render, gypsum plaster and vinyl paints, do not allow the cob to dry out after a spell of wet weather, so it gradually accumulates moisture until it eventually starts to crumble. Ensuring that any coating, internal and external, applied to the cob is moisture permeable is essential to the success of the wall.

So far as planning permission is concerned, cob wall buildings would be treated in exactly the same way as those with walls of masonry or timber-framed construction. The issues revolve around the appropriateness of the building in that location, design, finishes and the like, not with construction materials and methods. Compliance with the Building Regulations can be a different matter as it is likely that the building control officer will not have a great deal of knowledge on cob walls. It will probably be necessary to supply a lot more information than would otherwise be the case. The Plymouth University School of Earthen Architecture can help with soil analysis, thermal performance and the like.

Thermal performance can be a problem, but compliance with Building Regulation Approved Documents is not necessarily mandatory if another method can be shown to be as effective in achieving the desired end. Cob is well known for being a very comfortable material in which to live – in part, this is due to its excellent thermal properties, being a combination of high thermal resistance and thermal storage and good humidity regulation.

However, from a building regulation point of view only thermal resistance is taken into account. An 850mm thick cob wall (which is much thicker than a traditional cob wall) will give a thermal resistance of 0.45w/m/k, higher than the maximum of 0.35 allowed. A study carried

6

out by Equipe Matériaux et Thermique des Bâtiments, INSA de Rennes, France in 2004 concluded that the thermal behaviour of a 500mm thick cob wall is about the same as that of concrete block cavity wall with 75mm of insulation.

Many new cob structures have been built over the past few years, all with Building Regulations approval. Kevin McCabe's houses at Keppel Gate and the Cob Tun House, which won an RIBA award in 2005, are a couple of examples. The technical and thermal performance of the particular mix of cob needs to be evaluated, with regard to its density, shrinkage rate, and compressed strength. These, in turn, will dictate the thickness of foundations. Again the Plymouth University Centre for Earthen Architecture can help with this (for a reasonable fee).

Another issue to bear in mind is that cob walls offer very high thermal mass; they are good at storing heat, both internal and from the sun. As a result they do not heat quickly and cob houses do not perform well with instantaneous heating systems – particularly heated air. They take time to reach a comfortable temperature, but will maintain a constant temperature, irrespective of the vagaries of the weather.

Fortunately, the traditional skills, almost lost in the second half of the twentieth century, have been saved so that now there are professional suppliers and builders who are able to build structurally stable and aesthetically pleasing cob structures.

The Weald & Downland Open Air Museum run courses on cob construction, or get more information from :-

www.buildsomethingbeautiful.com

www.jjsharpe.co.uk

www.earthedworld.co.uk

www.abeysmallcombe.com

www.tech.plym.ac.uk/soa/arch/earth.htm 5634

www.cat.org.uk

STRAW-BALE HOUSES

In many respects straw-bale construction is very similar to cob. Both suffer if moisture penetrates, both require a 'good hat and a good pair of boots', both offer good thermal and sound insulation, and both require particular skills to build well.

6

Unlike cob, straw-bale construction is relatively new. It was first developed in the USA in the nineteenth century (when baling machines became more common) by pioneer farmers short of building materials. Straw, as a waste product from wheat production, was used as it was readily available, if not all that was available in the prairie states. Initially, buildings were intended to be temporary, until more substantial materials came to hand, but the straw house proved so comfortable and durable that the farmers decided to continue with them. The technology has not advanced much since those early days and, in truth, it is difficult to see how it could advance.

Using straw bales allows a greater flexibility in design. As with cob, curved walls are easy and interesting.

As with cob, water is a key factor in the straw-bale construction process. Cob starts wet and is allowed to dry, straw bales start dry and have to stay that way. If the moisture content gets over 20 percent, the straw will rot, with predictable consequences. On that note, if a straw-bale building fails structurally it tends to be fairy undramatic. It does not suddenly tumble in a cloud of rubble and dust, but rather it gently subsides as the straw gradually gives way to unsupportable compression.

The three big scares with straw bale are:

1. Fire. Straw is flammable and will burn. It is actually no greater fire risk than timber-frame construction with timber cladding. If the straw is lime rendered it has the same fire risk as masonry and passes all Building Regulations tests.
2. Durability. Straw is an insubstantial material and cannot last. Straw-bale houses built 100 years ago are still standing. As with all things, it is the care given to the construction detail that determines the durability of the building.
3. Vermin infestation. Straw will be a welcome home to rats and mice. However, rats and mice do not particularly like straw (although they do like hay) as it is a poor food source and poor nest material. In addition, they would have to chew through lime render to get at it. There is no more risk of vermin infestation than with any other construction method.

6

Straw is a relatively lightweight material and consequently foundations can be lighter. But the need to prevent rising damp reaching the straw tends to counteract this. As with cob, a plinth foundation wall of 300mm to 500mm above ground level is used to prevent rainwater splash. Straw does not 'wick', that is draw up moisture. Rising damp will not be drawn into the wall and rain will only penetrate as far as the wind drives it. Therefore, water penetration to the bottom and sides of the wall is less critical than penetration at the top.

Straw bales can either be used to form the structure of the building – to be load bearing, or as infill to an oversize timber frame. This last method is the one most approved by building societies and the only one likely to release a mortgage.

Load-bearing or Nebraska method

This is the original method pioneered by the Nebraskan farmers, from whom it derives its name. In this method, there is no structural framework and the bales themselves take the weight of the roof. They are placed together as brick or concrete blocks would be in a masonry wall and pinned to the foundations and to each other with wooden stakes – hazel is most commonly used in the UK. They have a wooden roof plate on the top course, again fastened to the bales with stakes and tied down to the foundations. The roof is then constructed on top of the roof plate. Typically, this is a cut-timber roof, but there is no impediment to using trusses. The roof covering is also a matter of choice, but it is often turf or thatch, which is probably more to do with enhancing eco credentials than because they are intrinsically better materials. Timber shingles or reclaimed slates would work just as well. Whatever the roof covering, an extra eaves overhang is needed, up to 600mm, to ensure there is no rainwater penetration to the top of the wall.

Windows and doors are placed inside structural timber-box frames, which are pinned into the bales with hazel stakes as the walls go up. To maintain stability and avoid bale-wobble, windows and door openings cannot take up more than 50 percent of the wall's surface area and a wall cannot be more than 6m long unbraced.

It is now common practice to bind the bales with wire straps as the walls go up to prevent bale wobble and help compress the bales until the roof is on. The weight of the roof tends to compress the bales and adds structural stability.

The advantage that this method has over other methods is that it is possible to learn how to build a bale wall fairly quickly and to undertake the construction as a DIY project. This is not only fun and satisfying but also saves money. Our standard house will need 400-500 bales at a cost of perhaps £2 to £2.50 per bale (delivered). Added to

6

this will be the cost of coppiced hazel stakes and the other timber of openings and wall plate – perhaps £1,000. A similar brick and block cavity wall will cost around £10,000 to build – and will not be as much fun to construct.

Lightweight timber frame

This design idea was developed by Barbara Jones of Amazon Nails – the definitive source of information on straw-bale building in the UK – to retain the benefits of the load-bearing style and enable the roof to be constructed before the straw walls are built. The importance of protection from the weather throughout the construction process cannot be over-emphasised. Even slightly damp bales will rot. It is common to erect a scaffolding tent over the whole site to make sure it is fully protected from the elements.

This method uses a lightweight timber framework that needs temporary bracing and props to give it stability until the straw is in place. The straw is an essential part of the structural integrity of the building, and still the main load-bearing element. Timber posts are located at corners and either side of window and door openings, and are designed such that the wall plate at first floor and/or roof level can be slotted down into them once the straw is in place, thus allowing for compression on the bales. Compression of the bales is essential for the stability of the wall. Walls are constructed in such a way that the wall plate and roof are kept 100mm above the finished straw wall height while the wall is being built. This allows for compressed settlement of the straw wall once the bracing and props are removed. A wall seven bales high will compress up to 50mm.

Post and beam

This is essentially the same as any other post and beam construction. A structurally stable timber frame is constructed, up to and including roof covering, and straw bales are used as infill to the walls. In this case, the straw takes no load bearing and is subject to less compression. As a result, the bales are less stable and need to be well pinned in to the frame.

This method is the one preferred by architects and building societies. Being essentially traditional post and beam, it is well understood and does not use what might be considered experimental construction methods.

Compared to either of the other methods it uses a lot of good-quality timber and requires a high level of carpentry skill. It is not really for the DIY builder. The timber used in the frame does not need to be top-quality oak or similar, as would usually be used in post and beam, as the frame is not exposed, but it still needs to be good-quality softwood.

6

Although more complex and expensive than the other methods, it brings all the flexibility advantages of post and beam, being more adaptable to extension or modification. The costs of taking down and rebuilding a straw wall is small.

Thermal performance

All straw-bale buildings share the same high levels of thermal resistance. Building Regulations require a U-value for external walls of 0.35. A typical bale of straw has a U-value of 0.13 – significantly better thermal performance than regulations require and as good as the much-vaunted German Passiv Haus standard with its high-tech, highly-insulated walls.

More information

The best source of information is Amazon Nails at www.strawbalefutures.org.uk who publish a very useful guide to building straw-bale houses and run regular courses on all the construction methods.

HEMP WALLS OR HEMCRETE

Using hemp as a building material is a fairly new idea. Hemp shiv (the waste product left when the more valuable hemp fibre is extracted from the plant) is mixed with a lime binder to produce a filling and insulation for timber-frame walls. This mix is generally known as hemcrete. A plywood shutter is fixed around the timber-frame wall and the hemcrete poured and rammed in place.

There is some discussion over whether hemcrete is a structural material or not. It is generally used as a single-wall construction of 300mm thick, at which thickness it is not strong enough to be structural and needs a timber frame for stability. Used in this way it removes the need for a second skin to the wall and the structural improvement it provides means that a lighter timber frame can be used – 100mm rather than 150mm, which would be usual for a single-skin timber-frame.

When the shutter is removed, the surface of the hemcrete is ready to accept a lime render, internally and externally, and finished with limewash. As with other natural materials, hemcrete is a breathing material and needs breathable finishes to allow moisture to dissipate. Another effect of this is to move moisture away from the timber frame, protecting it from decaying influences and increasing its longevity.

6

Most importantly, hemcrete provides excellent thermal performance. The actual thermal resistance will vary with the mix, proportions of hemp to lime, but approximate U-values are:

300mm wall 0.29 W/m²K 400mm wall 0.22 W/m²K 500mm wall 0.18 W/m²K

Remembering that the Building Regulations Part L call for a maximum U-value of 0.35, even 300mm is a 30 percent improvement and 500mm is Passiv Haus standard.

A result of combining lime and hemp is to allow it to act as a carbon sink. As the hemp grows it absorbs CO_2, which would normally be released as the plant decays. Mixing with lime prevents, or at least delays, the decay and data from Lime Technology Ltd suggest that 50kg of CO_2 can be locked up per 1m² of hemcrete walling (at 300mm thick), which in addition to embodied energy savings is a useful one-off carbon saving.

This one-off skewing of the carbon cycle is a useful bonus, using materials that 'lock in' carbon in its unoxidised state, and preserve it there, warm and dry, for the foreseeable future. This may only be a postponement of its inevitable rotting or burning, but it is postponed for at least the life of the building. Hemcrete, like most natural materials, is eminently recyclable. The hemcrete can be broken up, mix with more lime binder and reused. So the delay in releasing the locked-in carbon could go on for quite a long time.

The argument applies equally to all plant materials and can be extended to using as much timber as possible for construction. It is also the best, possibly only, sound argument for paper recycling.

More information

Lhoist UK Ltd www.lhoist.com
The Hemp Lime Construction Products www.hemplime.org.uk
Ralph Carpenter, Modece Architects, Bury St Edmunds.

FURTHER OPTIONS

The three methods discussed are, perhaps, the most popular options. Cob has a long tradition stretching back 500 years and is being actively revived. Straw is a comparative newcomer having been around only 100 years. It has a good deal of enthusiastic support as it is a material that is readily available, easy to work with and it locks in CO_2. Hemcrete is a very new idea (using old materials), and brings together many of the benefits of the other two. But there are more options:

6

JEREMY PHILLIPS

Cob incorporates site soil and locally sourced clay, with straw acting as the binding ingredient.

Rammed earth- As the name implies, earth is rammed into a shutter to form the wall. Very similar to cob, but tends to be used in chalky soils and is rammed dry.

Cob blocks- Again, as the name implies, cob is a clay and straw mix in block form. These have been produced for many years principally as a repair material for pre-existing cob buildings. New build with cob block is gaining popularity as it provides all the advantages of cob, but without the labour-intensive construction process (but with proportionately higher cost).

Clay blocks- There is a good deal of research into unfired clay blocks by people like Hanson, Ibstock and Plymouth University, and, as such, it seems to have the backing to make it as a 'standard' building method. It is similar in many ways to the clay lump or 'adobe', the universal mudbrick. Adobe is found mostly in East Anglia where it has been used since the end of the 18th century. Construction is similar to brickwork with regular bonded courses,

6

but the dried blocks are much larger and are usually laid in a mortar of clay, rendered over with more clay or, more usually, lime.

Wattle and daub- This is a method that everybody learnt about at school. Most usually, wattle and daub is used as infill to a post and beam structure. A woven panel of oak or hazel (the wattle) is fixed in place and daubed with a mixture of clay or earth with straw and dung. It does not really have anything going for it as it is non-structural, a poor insulator, labour intensive and uses a lot of dung.

CONCLUSION

With our increased awareness of the effect we have on the planet, it is perhaps not surprising that there is a burgeoning movement to construct our homes from materials that are from the earth, using methods that are simple, non invasive and self reliant. They are all ancient methods, in some cases modified by modern understanding and technology; in others, they are exactly as they have always been.

The fact that they work in providing comfortable, affordable housing has been proven over centuries. The fact that they present problems in meeting regulations says more about the blinkered thinking of the regulation setters than it does about the materials and methods.

Are they just a dream? That depends on how determined you are.

7 APPENDICES

1. WHAT IS THE LEGISLATION?

For the time being at least, building a low-energy home is, for the self builder, a matter of choice, and there is no legislation around building sustainably.

Planning Policy Statement 22 (in England) and Technical Advice Note 8 (in Wales) requires or suggests that developments of 10 or more domestic properties produce at least 10 percent of their energy needs on site. Some local authorities, most notably Merton, have decided to increase this minimum requirement to as much as 25 percent and this minimum requirement is likely to be embodied in statute in 2008 (as not enough local authorities are taking it up voluntarily). Ruth Kelly has stated, on behalf of the Government, that all new homes built after 2016 (2012 in Wales) have zero carbon emissions and groups are forming all over England and Wales to discuss how this can be achieved. So far no answers have come forth. The plan is to rack-up the minimum requirements under Building Regulations Part L1A on a three-year cycle until zero carbon emissions are reached in 2016. By that time, Wales is likely to be independent of English Building Regulations (as Scotland already is) and will have set their own standards.

It seems unlikely that this movement will be reversed so the expectation has to be that achieving low-energy housing for all house builders, and those carrying out major renovations and extensions, will become compulsory. The only questions are when and how much?

The Building Research Establishment (BRE) produce a booklet called The Green Guide to Housing Specification that lists and grades materials used in house construction. BRE are also responsible for drafting the Building Regulations on behalf of the Government and for producing the Ecohomes standard and The Code for Sustainable Homes. Currently, there is no legislation around using sustainable

7

materials in private house construction, merely encouragement in the form of these two standards. However, housing associations and any housing receiving local or central Government funding have to achieve at least the Good (2-star) standard under Ecohomes.

As has been shown, there is at least 44 tonnes of CO_2 embodied in the materials of the average house. Under 2007 Part L standards, this amounts to nine years of CO_2 emissions. It does not take a great leap of imagination to conclude that we can look forward to legislation around the sourcing and energy content of the materials we use.

2. EXAMPLE SAP CALCULATIONS

The Standard Assessment Procedure (SAP) was devised by the Government as a means of assessing the energy performance of a building. The SAP calculation gives a rating of 1 to 100 and is determined by calculating the Target Emissions Rate (TER) and the Dwelling Emission Rate (DER). The TER is calculated based on a notional building of exactly the same size and shape as the actual dwelling that conforms to the minimum energy performance requirements of the 2002 Part L1a, less 20 percent. So the new dwellings must be 20 percent more efficient than the previous minimum standards of 2002 Part L1A.

The DER is calculated from the design specification of the house in question (at the design stage, so it is not the actual emission rate) and both figures are given in kg of CO_2 per m² of usable floor area. To demonstrate compliance, the DER must be less than the TER and this constitutes a pass or fail of regulations 17A and 17B, and thereby a pass or fail of Part L1 as a whole.

The DER is affected by the following factors:
- **Air permeability**
- **Heating and ventilation systems**
- **Insulation**
- **Element U-values**
- **Renewable energy**
- **Glazing**

It is possible to trade one off against another to achieve the desired DER figure, and there is a good software tool to help with this at www.playtheregs.com. It is very easy to use, and free, but it is not definitive and only provides an idea of what can be done. Ultimately, a SAP calculation provided by an approved SAP assessor showing an appropriate DER figure is needed to comply with the regulation.

7

SAMPLE SAP WORKSHEET

**SAP 2005 WORKSHEET FOR DWELLING AS DESIGNED
(Version 9.80, October 2005)
CALCULATION OF DWELLING EMISSIONS FOR REGULATION
COMPLIANCE
APPROVED DOCUMENT L1A, 2006 EDITION**
calculated by program BRESAP version 4.24j, printed on June 16, 2007

File name – Plot 1, The Street, The Town

Plot 1, The Street

1. Overall dwelling dimensions	Area m²)	Av Storey (height (m)	Volume (m³)
Ground Floor	131.02	2.40	314.45
First Floor	113.40	2.50	283.50
Total Floor Area	244.42		
Dwelling Volume			597.95

2. Ventilation Rate		m3 per hour	
Number of chimneys	1 x 40	40	
Number of flues	1 x 20	20	
Number of fans or passive vents	7 x 10	70	
Number of flueless gas fires	0 x 40	0	
			ACH
Infiltration due to chimneys, flues and fans			0.22
Pressure test	Yes		
Measured/design q50	8.0		
Infiltration rate			0.62
Number of sides sheltered	0		
Shelter factor	1.00		
Adjusted infiltration rate			0.62
(Natural ventilation)			
Effective air change rate			0.69

3. Heat losses and heat loss parameter			
Element	Area (m²)	U-value (W/m²K)	A x U (W/K)
Doors	5.00	2.20	11.00
Windows (1)	22.00	(1.80)1.68	36.94
Windows (2)	10.50	(1.80)1.68	17.63
Ground Floor	131.02	0.15	19.65

3. Heat losses and heat loss parameter

Sample SAP Worksheet

7

3. Heat losses and heat loss parameter (CONTINUED)

Element	Area (m^2)	U-value (W/m^{2}K)	A x U (W/K)
Walls (1)	22.54	0.20	4.51
Walls (2)	92.11	0.19	17.50
Walls (3)	51.34	0.19	9.75
Roof (1)	113.40	0.13	14.74
Roof (2)	21.74	0.16	3.48
Total area of elements	469.63		
Fabric heat loss			135.20
Thermal bridges (0.80 x total area)			37.57
Total fabric heat loss			172.77
Ventilation heat loss			136.27
Heat loss coefficient			309.27
Heat loss parameter			1.26

4. Water heating energy requirements

	kWh/year
Energy content of heated water	3540
Distribution loss	625
Cylinder volume	160
Cylinder loss factor (kWh/litre/day)	0.0181
Volume factor	0.909
Temperature factor	0.54
Energy loss from cylinder in kWh/year (160 litre)	518
Primary circuit loss	360
Total	5043
Solar input	0
Output from water heating	5043
Heat gains form water heating	2087

5. Internal gains   Watts

Lights, appliances, cooking and metabolic	1199
Reduction in lighting gains	- 56
Additional gains (Table 5a)	10
Water heating	238
Total internal gains	1391

Sample SAP Worksheet

7

6. Solar gains Orientation	Area		Flux g	FF	Shading	Gains (W)	
Northeast (1)	0.9 x	18.34	34	0.63	0.7	0.54	134
Southeast (1)	0.9 x	3.66	64	0.63	0.7	0.54	50
Southwest (2)	0.9 x	10.50	64	0.63	0.7	0.54	144
Total							328
Total gains							1719
Gain/loss ratio							5.56
Utilisation factor							0.96
Useful gains							1651

7. Mean internal temperature	°C
Mean temperature of living area	18.88
Temperature adjustment from Table 4e	0.00
Adjustment gains	0.27
Adjusted living area temperature	19.15
Temperature difference between zones	1.84
Living area fraction	0.14
Rest-of-house area fraction	0.86
Mean internal temperature	17.57

8. Degree days	
Temperature rise from gains	5.34
Base temperature	12.22
Degree days	1391.80

9. Energy requirement	kWh/year
Space heating requirement (useful)	10323
Fraction of heat from secondary system	0.10
Efficiency of main heating system	90.70
Efficiency of secondary heating system	65
Space heating (main)	10244
Space heating (secondary)	1588
Water heating requirement	5043
Efficiency of water heater	90.70
Water heating fuel	5560
Electricity for pumps and fans	175

Sample SAP Worksheet

10.	Does not apply		
11.	Does not apply		

12. Carbon dioxide emissions	Energy (kWh/year)	Emissions factor	Emissions (kg/year)
Space heating (main)	10244	0.194	1987
Space heating (secondary)	1588	0.025	40
Water heating	5560	0.194	1079
Space and water heating			3106
Pumps and fans	175	0.422	74
Electricity for lighting	2110	0.422	890
Electricity generated – PV	0	0.568	0
Electricity generated – CHP	0	0.568	0
Total CO2 emissions			4070
			kg/m2/year
Dwelling Carbon Dioxide Emission Rate (DER)			**16.65**

NOTE: This worksheet is produced by the SAP assessor and is typically NOT given to the client. It is, at best, difficult to understand and, as many of the calculations and coefficients are done in the background, it is also difficult to penetrate. It leads to the final figure, the DER which is the only figure of any real importance, although the CO_2 emissions at a little over four tonnes pa is of interest.

SAMPLE OF SAP 2005 CHECKLIST

REGULATION COMPLIANCE CHECKLIST – APPROVED DOCUMENT L1A, 2006 EDITION
ASSESSED BY PROGRAM BRESAP VERSION 4.24J

PLOT 1, THE STREET

DWELLING AS DESIGNED

1 TER and DER

Fuel for main heating system	Mains gas (fuel factor = 1.00)	**OK**
Target CO_2 emission rate	TER = 18.23 kg/m^2	
Dwelling CO_2 emission rate	DER = 16.65 kg/m^2	

Sample SAP 2005 checklist continued

7

2.1 Fabric U-values

Element	Average	Highest	
Wall	0.19 (max 0.35)	0.20 (max 0.70)	OK
Floor	0.15 (max 0.25)	0.15 (max 0.70)	OK
Roof	0.13 (max 0.25)	0.16 (max 0.35)	OK
Openings	1.85 (max 2.20)	0.20 (max 3.30	OK

2.2 Common areas — Builder's submissions

2.3 Heating efficiency

Main heating system	Boiler system with radiators or underfloor	
	Baxi Heating Barcelona	
	Efficiency: 90.7%	
	Minimum: 86.0%	OK
Secondary heating system	Room heaters – wood	
	Closed room heater	
	Efficiency: 65%	
	Minimum: 65%	OK

2.4 Cylinder insulation

Hot water storage	Nominal cylinder loss: 2.63 kWh/day	
	Permitted by DHCG : 2.73	OK
Primary pipework insulated:	Yes	OK

2.5 Controls

Space heating controls	Timer and temperature zone control	OK
Hot water controls	Cylinderstat	OK
	Boiler interlock	OK
	Independent timer for DHW	OK

2.6 Other provisions for heating for heating

Builder's submissions

2.7 Fixed internal & external lighting

Builder's submissions

Sample SAP 2005 checklist continued

7

3.1 Summertime temperature

Overheating risk (SE England)	Medium	**OK**
Based on:		
Thermal mass parameter	5.33	
Overshading	More than average	
Glazing facing Northeast	18.43m², no overhang	
Glazing facing Southeast	3.66 m², no overhang	
Glazing facing Southwest	10.50 m², no overhang	
Ventilation rate	0.93	
Blinds/curtains	Light coloured roller blind, closed 25% of daylight hours	

4.1 Key features

Wall U-value 0.20
Wall U-value 0.19
Wall U-value 0.19
Floor U-value 0.15
Roof U-value 0.13
Main heating efficiency 90.7

4.2 Accredited details — Builder's submissions

4.3 Non-accredited details — Builder's submissions

4.4 Site inspection checks — Builder's submissions

4.5 Design air permeability

Design air permeability at 50 Pascal's:	8.00	**OK**

4.6 Sample pressure tests — Builder's submissions

4.7 Commissioning — Builder's submissions

Overall Result: **PASS**

5.1 Provision of information

O&M instructions	Builder's submissions
SAP rating	**SAP = 80**

7

The previous two pages are what would normally be made available to the client by the SAP Assessor. Box I shows the DER is less than the TER and therefore constitutes the PASS in Overall Results. The remainder of the information goes towards determining the SAP rating, in this case 80 out of 100, which is a reasonably good score by modern standards.

A full copy of the SAP specification, setting out exactly what is assessed and how, is available at www.bre.co.uk/sap2005. The document is 74 pages long, very difficult reading and goes to show that this is perhaps a misleading, not to say misconceived, way of assessing the energy performance of a house. It should also be noted that this assessment method only applies to houses of less than 450m^2, larger houses are assessed using standards set for commercial buildings, which are becoming ever more stringent.

The particular version of SAP software used in this example does not provide an Environmental Impact Rating (EIR). This is based on the CO_2 emissions associated with space heating, water heating, ventilation and lighting. It is also rated I to 100 with 100 being the best score. The EIR does not directly affect compliance with the regulation as the CO_2 figures are taken into the SAP rating via the fuels, U-values and efficiency of equipment.

In summary, SAP 2005 is a compliance requirement that serves little useful function for the sustainable builder. The problem with it is that there is a danger that a PASS is considered good enough. For the sustainable builder, a PASS is little more than a starting point.

3. BUILDING REGULATIONS 2006

A complete version of the Building Regulations is downloadable from
www.planningportal.gov.uk/england/professionals/en/1115314110382.html
It is published as a series of Approved Documents which provide explanation and guidance around the meeting the regulations and breaks the full regulations down into the following parts:

- **Preparing for flood**
- **Basements for dwellings**
- **Broadband**
- **Part A – Structural safety**
- **Part B – Fire safety**
- **Part C – Resistance to moisture and weather**
- **Part D – Toxic substances**
- **Part E – Resistance to sound**
- **Part F – Ventilation**
- **Part G – Hygiene**
- **Part H – Drainage and waste disposal**
- **Part J – Heat producing appliances**
- **Part K – Prevention from falling**
- **Part L – Conservation of fuel and power**
- **Part M – Access to and use of buildings**
- **Part N – Glazing safety**
- **Part P – Electrical safety**

The sections relevant to energy and sustainability for the house builder (and those carrying out major renovations) are Part C, Part F and Part LIA.

The current version was published in April 2006, and is a revision of the Building Regulations 2000, which is the base document upon which all amendments are set. The new Part L requires a step up of around 10 percent in the energy efficiency of new builds on the previous Part L and it now also applies to major extensions and renovations as well as new build. A major extension is generally considered to be more than 50 percent of the pre-existing floor area and a major renovation to be one that requires works to the fabric of the building envelope (walls, floor and roof) but not just decorative work.

Among many other things it increases insulation levels, requires improved air tightness and increases the proportion of energy-efficient light fittings.

7

PRÉCIS OF PART C

Part C deals with the Resistance to Moisture and Weather. So far as the sustainable builder is concerned it has a couple of effects.

The regulations require that the fabric of the building resist the penetration of water (rain or other precipitation – not flood water) through the roof, the top of an external wall, the bottom of an external wall and from the external surface of an external wall to the internal surface. At first glance, no one would argue with any of this, we need to keep the rain out. But for a straw-bale, cob, post and beam or any single-skin wall construction, including the renovation of a stone barn, it presents problems.

Water penetration through the roof and at the top of the wall is, in all cases, to be strongly resisted. Penetration from the bottom of the external wall, and from the external surface to the internal surface is another matter.

Take the case of converting a stone barn (that may have stood doing its job, being wind and water tight for 200 years). The walls will be single-skin stone, maybe 450mm to 800mm thick. The stone is likely to be laid in a lime mortar and the design of the wall is to **allow** rain-water to penetrate and to drain out of the bottom of the wall into the ground. It was recognised 200 years ago that lime and to a greater or lesser extent, stone, are porous and that it is impossible to prevent rain water penetrating. The design did not have a damp-proof course at the bottom of the wall (although this technology existed 200 years ago and was used) as this would prevent the moisture draining out. The regulation insists that an injected damp-proof course be incorporated, irrespective of the fact that this will hold water in the wall and encourage it to exit via the **internal** surface.

This rationale holds true for any single-skin construction being more of a problem for some construction methods – straw bale, cob, post and beam – than others – single-skin timber-frame, single-skin block. The irony is that the majority of building control officers seem to recognise that it is an anomaly but feel bound to enforce the regulation.

A strict interpretation of the regulation will also not allow lime render as a weather-proofing coating as lime is, by its nature, permeable, which is why it is being used.

PRÉCIS OF PART F

Regulation F1 states that: "There shall be adequate means of ventilation provided for the people in the building." There then follows a 53-page document setting out what 'adequate' means, and how to achieve it.

The regulation, like all the regulations, deals with all types of buildings from houses to factories and the ventilation requirements vary hugely with the type of building and what is going on in there. Factories can produce all sorts of pollutants, offices more than enough body-odour, restaurant kitchens excessive heat or moisture. The regulations have to deal with all these potential extreme conditions.

The house builder has to deal with just three issues:

1. Extraction from kitchen, bathrooms and utility rooms
2. Fresh air infiltration to habitable rooms
3. Meeting the air permeability standard set out in Part L1A

There are two basic methods of achieving this:

Infiltration- This is perhaps the normal method of extractor fans and trickle vents. The regulations allow for windows to be opened to provide what is called 'purge ventilation'. That is the removal of extraordinary pollutants from, say, decorating or burning the dinner.

Extractor fans have to be fitted to the kitchen, bathrooms and utility room and minimum standards are set.

Typically intermittent extractors are used (those that are only switched on when necessary) and in the kitchen need to have a minimum capacity of 60 litres per second (l/s) or 30l/s if it is a cooker hood. Bathrooms need a minimum of 15l/s, as does a utility room. A WC (not in a bathroom) only needs 6l/s. The purpose of all these is to remove moisture and odour.

In addition, habitable rooms must allow outside air in, to refresh the internal air and to replace that air extracted. In the case of bathrooms, kitchens and utility rooms a 10mm gap on the bottom of the door is sufficient, for other habitable rooms a trickle vent is fitted, usually over the window. The regulations set a minimum height of 1.7m above floor level for the avoidance of draughts. Calculating the size of trickle vents is a complex process. It is based on the permeability of the building at 50 Pascals and the infiltration needs to be at least 1/20th of the air leakage rate. (Air leakage is measured under positive pressure and infiltration is at normal atmospheric pressure – which explains the difference.) In addition, the size of the

7

room being ventilated is taken into consideration. The answer is to consult with the window supplier and/or architect who should be familiar with ventilation rates, trickle vents and the regulations.

Controllable ventilation- Mechanical ventilation systems, with or without heat recovery. If the regulations in Part L are stepped up as planned from the existing $10m^2$/hr to $3m^2$ per hour, mechanical ventilation will become essential. At below $5m^2$/hr there is insufficient air leaking into the house to dilute or remove the exhalation CO_2 and provide breathable air.

The minimum requirement is a ventilation rate of 0.3l/s per m^2 of internal floor area, which applies whatever type of ventilation system is installed.

The purpose of this regulation is to place emphasis on the need to control the ventilation. It follows from the air permeability regulations that if the rate at which air leaves the building is to be limited to provide greater thermal efficiency then the rate at which air enters the building must also be controlled. Mechanical ventilation systems not only control the amount of air entering the building, they can also control the moisture content, pollutants, pollen, and even the temperature. All of which are, of course, essential if the interior of the building is sealed off from the outside world.

Designing these systems is another complex business and will vary with the design of the house. The Approved Document provides guidance, but it is a matter best left to the experts. There are plenty of Mechanical Ventilation and Heat Recovery systems suppliers able to assist. It should be kept in mind that these systems seldom work well in retrofit situations. They need to be designed to the building and installed in the fabric of the building. Which is possible in a new build or a major renovation, but seldom otherwise.

PASSIVE STACK VENTILATION

This is a whole house ventilation system that relies on pressure differential, internal to external, to draw air from the building. It does not use fans but ducting is installed to each room in the house (normally mounted on the ceiling) and connected to a roof stack. There is a basic requirement to have a long stack over a warm, wet room, which allows convection currents to gain momentum and overcome external air pressure. Wind passing over the stack draws air from the ducts and thereby from the rooms (exactly the same principle as a chimney over a fire).

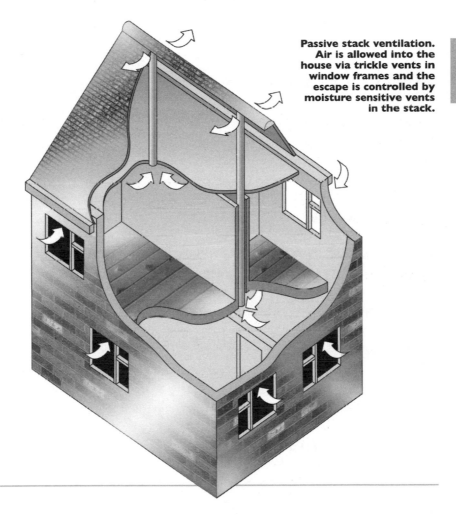

Passive stack ventilation. Air is allowed into the house via trickle vents in window frames and the escape is controlled by moisture sensitive vents in the stack.

7

The BRE Innovation Park at Watford has an office building ventilated with a PSV with the stack built on the outside of the building. The external surface of the stack is made from glass bricks, which allows the sun to warm the air in the stack and create stronger convection currents.

The system is becoming very popular with sustainable builders and is used extensively on the BedZED development, for instance. Designed properly they provide effective ventilation with no energy input. Again, design is the key issue and it will vary with each building. The Part F Approved Document provides guidance on design and installation but it is really a matter for the experts. As with mechanical ventilation, it is difficult to install effectively in a renovation or refurbishment.

7 PRÉCIS OF PART L1A

TARGET CO$_2$ EMISSION RATE

The TER is the minimum energy performance requirement for new dwellings approved by the Secretary of State in accordance with Regulation 17B. It is expressed in units of kg/m^2 of floor area per year emitted as a result of the provision of heating, hot water, ventilation and internal fixed lighting for a 'standardised' household.

The calculation of the TER is a part of the SAP 2005 calculation and can only be done by software approved by BRE.

CALCULATING THE CO$_2$ EMISSIONS FROM THE ACTUAL DWELLING

This is the DER and again forms part of the SAP 2005 calculation and can only be done with approved software. Although they use the term 'actual dwelling', they mean the dwelling at the design and specification stage. All the data used in the calculation is taken from the drawings and specification, including the anticipated air permeability. There is a reliance on the builder and the building control officer to check that the building is built as specified, with the exception of air permeability when a test certificate must be produced.

SECONDARY HEATING

If secondary heating, or provision for secondary heating (for example, a fireplace) is specified, it is assumed to be used and contribute a minimum of 10 percent to the overall space heating. It forms part of the DER calculation and the efficiency of the equipment to be installed is applied to the fuel used. The worst case is to not specify the equipment. So that if the drawings show a chimney and the specification states that there is a gas connection adjacent to the chimney but does not state which gas fire is to be installed, SAP calculation assumes that a gas fire will be fitted, that it will use the chimney and therefore have an efficiency of 20 percent, with consequently devastating effect on the CO$_2$ emission rate.

7

LIGHTING

The regulation requires that a minimum of 25 percent of all fixed light fittings are specifically for low-energy lighting. That means that those fittings will not accept bayonet cap or Edison-screw lamps. In ALL cases the DER is calculated using a fixed assumption of 30 percent low-energy lighting irrespective of the number of low-energy light fittings actually specified. This is done so that lighting is not tradable, so the builder cannot increase the proportion of low-energy lamps and offset this against poorer insulation.

ACHIEVING THE TARGET

Achieving the target means achieving a good DER and this section deals with the potential impact of installing renewable energy systems and how they can be a more cost-effective option than increasing insulation or improving air permeability. The way that U-values are used means that, however big the renewable energy system installed, it will not compensate for a poor building envelope.

DESIGN LIMITS FOR ENVELOPE STANDARDS

The technical guidance to the Regulations state: 'To achieve the TER, the envelope standards for most of the elements will need to be significantly better than those set out in the following paragraphs.'

U-VALUES
BR 443 sets out a convention for calculating U-values and sets limits for each element of:

	Area weighted	Limiting
Wall	0.35	0.70
Floor	0.25	0.70
Roof	0.25	0.35
Windows and doors	2.20	3.3

The area-weighted figure is the one usually used and the one quoted on insulation and other products. In practice, these figures have to be improved on to achieve a good DER (in the SAP example shown, the figures are walls 0.20, floor 0.15, roof 0.16, windows and doors 2.20).

7

AIR PERMEABILITY

'A reasonable limit for the design air permeability is $10m^3/h/m^2$ at 50Pa.' Which may or may not be a good thing (see Section 2 – Insulation). The major problem with this issue is that it is calculated at the design stage and the SAP rating (and Pass or Fail) is based on the design air permeability. The actual permeability **must** be tested (by independent testers) and the design rate achieved. Testing is not, and cannot be, carried out until the building is complete. The obvious consequence is that failure to meet the designed air rating will result in expensive remedial work.

The Regulations do allow a get-out clause. If the specification calls for a design air permeability of **$15m^3/h/m^2$**, then testing is not required. However, if this route is taken, then good insulation and/or renewable energy will be essential to achieve an acceptable DER.

DESIGN LIMITS FOR FIXED BUILDING SERVICES

Heating and hot water systems

In terms of traditional heating systems, nothing less than a condensing boiler with an efficiency rating of more than 86 percent will produce figures to enable a good DER. Heat pumps and biomass boilers will both qualify.

Insulation of pipes, ducts and vessels

This relates to the primary heating pipes (flow and return), ducting to mechanical ventilation and hot water storage tanks. In effect, all of these items have to insulated to the manufacturer's specification – which is usually 15mm of pipe lagging.

Mechanical ventilation

This sets out minimum standards for the provision of mechanical ventilation. So far as extract fans are concerned it is largely complied with by the manufacturers. Similarly, manufacturers of heat recovery systems ensure their products comply. The real question is by how much they exceed the regulation.

7

The minimum requirements are:

Specific fan power (SPF) for continuous extract	- 0.8 litres/s.W
SPF for balanced systems (mechanical ventilation)	- 2.0 litres/s.W
Heat recovery efficiency	- 66%

Mechanical cooling

On the basis that no house in the UK with any pretensions to sustainability will have air conditioning, this section is omitted. If you need air conditioning you have got the design wrong and need to start again.

Fixed internal lighting

To provide compliance at least 25 percent (but not more than 30 percent are counted) of the light fittings in habitable spaces (not cupboards) must be dedicated low-energy fittings. That is fittings that will not accept bayonet cap or Edison screw lamps. Both fluorescent and compact fluorescent lamps qualify.

A slight anomaly in the regulations is that these dedicated fittings are generally B-rated in efficiency terms, having a luminosity of perhaps 40 lumens per circuit watt. It is possible to buy Edison-screw and bayonet-cap compact fluorescent lamps with luminosity of 52 to 60 lumens per circuit watt and A-rated but that do not comply.

Fixed external lighting

This is defined as lighting that is fixed to the external surface of the dwelling and supplied from the occupier's electrical system. There are two options available:

1. Lamps that are not more than 150w and that have PIR movement and daylight controls.
2. Lamps that are more than 40 lumens per circuit watt (the same as used internally).

Lighting NOT fixed to an external surface of the dwelling, for example, lighting to the drive, garden lights, etc. are not covered by this regulation and there are plenty of solar-powered options available.

Limiting the effects of solar gains in summer

The purpose of this regulation is to limit the use of air conditioning (See mechanical cooling above). Solar heat gains form part of the SAP calculation and are a factor of the size and

7

orientation of windows and the amount of shading. The installation of high thermal mass in front of the windows will also be a factor by allowing heat to be absorbed.

The light-tight structures currently being advocated, together with low levels of air movement and high levels of insulation tend to use lots of glass to reduce the load on the heating system. It is very easy to go too far, or to plan poorly for summer conditions and find the house intolerably hot. The use of glass to encourage passive solar heat gains is a good idea but the design needs to incorporate shading in some form for the summer months.

The shading can be internal or external, curtains or blinds, fixed or moveable, or indeed natural (deciduous trees planted an appropriate distance from the house).

If reducing the amount of glass is taken as a measure to reduce the solar heat gain, the design may run foul of the requirements for minimum daylighting.

QUALITY OF CONSTRUCTION – BUILDING FABRIC

The regulation concerns itself with only two issues:
1. The insulation be reasonably continuous over the whole building envelope.
2. The air permeability be within reasonable limits.

Continuity of insulation

This section refers to the avoidance of thermal bridges (see Section 2), and for the first time appears in the Regulations. It sets out that insulation must overlap at joints in building elements (for example, floor and wall) and at the edges of elements such as around window and door openings.

In addition, the builder has to demonstrate that there is an adequate inspection system in place to ensure that the insulation is installed as specified. This effectively removes the burden from the building control officer and places it on the builder.

Air permeability and pressure testing

(See Air permeability on p152). This section goes to some length to determine what must be tested and how it is to be done.

What comes from this section is that failing the pressure test does not automatically mean failing Part L if the measured test result is better than 10m² per hour and the TER is still met. In reality, if the design calls for low permeability there was a reason for it and failing to meet the design requirement means that the design fails, even if it passes Part L. To put it another way, if the design is for a light-tight structure, the builder has to be sure to achieve it, and that means two things:

1. Far more attention to construction detail than the average builder is used to, and
2. A return to wet plastering (board and skim is not air-tight as skim cracks and cracks leak).

Alternative to pressure testing on small developments

A small development is defined as one with no more than two dwellings. In this case there are two options:

1. Demonstrate that a dwelling of the same design has been constructed by the same builder within the previous 12 months and that the dwelling passed the pressure test.
2. Adopt an air permeability of 15m² in the SAP calculation.

COMMISSIONING OF HEATING AND HOT WATER SYSTEMS

The regulation requires that heating and hot water systems are commissioned by a suitably qualified person to certificate that the plant and system is working in accordance with the manufacturer's specification.

OPERATING AND MAINTENANCE INSTRUCTIONS

This regulation is given the same weight as all those foregoing. The requirement is that the builder provides a manual that sets out sufficient information about the building and its fixed services (heating, ventilation and lighting) and their maintenance so that the building can be operated in a way as to use no more fuel than is reasonable. The manual must give specific reference to the systems and equipment actually installed in the building, rather than generic equipment of a similar type. This information then forms part of the new Home Information Pack and must also include the SAP rating.

4. A PRÉCIS OF THE ECOHOMES STANDARD

A complete version of the Ecohomes standard is downloadable from www.ecohomes.org. In April 2007, the code for Sustainable Homes replaced Ecohomes for new housing in England. Ecohomes 2006 will continue to be used for refurbished (or renovated) housing in England and for all housing in Scotland and Wales.

The Ecohomes standard is a step beyond Part L and moves from simple energy efficiency to a level of sustainability, dealing with all the principal issues:

- **Energy**
- **Transport**
- **Pollution**
- **Materials**
- **Water**
- **Land use and ecology**
- **Health and wellbeing**
- **Management**

The standard has been devised by Buildings Research Establishment to 'balance environmental performance with the need for a high quality of life and a safe and healthy internal environment.' Points are awarded for a level of attainment in each category so that the standard is not a simple pass or fail but properties are rated through a fairly complex assessment process from Pass to Good, Very Good and Excellent.

Points are awarded for each element of the standard with greater weighting given to some areas. Equally, some areas are easier to deal with than others. For instance, 1.83 points are awarded for installing all A-rated white goods (fridge, freezer, washing machine etc.) and virtually the same, 1.82 points, for reducing surface water run off. The first will probably be done as a matter of course, with only a trivial cost implication and the second will require thought, planning and not inconsiderable cost.

The assessment is carried out at the design stage and the normal process is for the owner/builder to decide what rating they want to achieve (Pass to Excellent) and use the services of an Ecohomes assessor to scrutinise the drawings and specification and suggest how best to achieve the desired rating. The maximum number of points available for each element is shown to give an idea of the influence of each element.

THE ECOHOMES ELEMENTS

7

ENERGY – 22 POINTS

Ene 1 – Dwelling emission rate – this is taken directly from the SAP 2005 calculation. The base level represents a normal condensing boiler and an increasing number of points are awarded up to 'true zero carbon solutions,' which is actually a DER of $-10kg/m^2/year$, which can only be achieved by generating more power than the house actually consumes.

Ene 2 – Building-envelope performance – points are awarded for the ability of the building fabric to resist the transference of heat. The Heat Loss Parameter is also a function to the SAP calculation, which is essentially a very good U-value.

Ene 3 – Drying space – points awarded for the provision of space (internal or external) for the drying of laundry.

Ene 4 – Eco labelled white goods – points for installing A-rated white goods, or if no white goods are installed, points for providing the occupier with information on Eco labelling (seems too easy, but it's true).

Ene 5 – Internal lighting – points for dedicated low-energy lighting (fittings that will only accept compact fluorescent lamps), above Part L requirement.

Ene 6 – External lighting – points for dedicated low-energy lighting and intruder lighting fitted with PIR and daylight sensors.

TRANSPORT – 8 POINTS

Tra 1 – Public transport – points for building variously within 500m or 1000m of public transport links. More points for a more frequent service (obviously outside the control of the builder but intended to encourage development close to links).

Tra 2 – Cycle storage – points for providing a lockable cycle store on the property.

Tra 3 – Local amenities – as with Tra 1, points for building within 500m or 1000m of local shops, post office, etc.

Tra 4 – Home office – points for including a home office within the property. Not as onerous as it sounds as a Home Office is defined as being space for a desk with dedicated power outlets and telephone connections.

POLLUTION – 10 POINTS

Pol 1 – Insulation ODP and GWP – points for using insulation materials with an ozone depletion potential (ODP) of zero and a global warming potential (GWP) of less than five. These materials are listed in the BRE Green Guide to Housing Specification.

7

Pol 2 – NOx emissions - NOx, or nitrogen oxide, is given off by the burning of fossil fuels. The amount of NOx for any piece of equipment is stated in the manufacturer's specification for that equipment. Increasing points are awarded for reducing NOx emissions.

Pol 3 – Reduction of surface run-off – Points awarded for reducing the amount of rainwater running into the sewer system.

Pol 4 – Renewable and Low Emission Energy Source – Needs a feasibility study into the potential efficacy of renewable energy and the implementation of that feasibility study.

Pol 5 – Flood risk mitigation – Points for the building being in a low flood-risk area or, in a medium flood-risk area, when the floor level of the building and car parking is above the predicted flood level.

MATERIALS – 14 POINTS

Mat 1 – Environmental impact of materials – points for using materials from the Green Guide for Housing Specification.

Mat 2 – Responsible sourcing of materials, basic building elements – looking at the main elements of the building (floors, walls, roof, etc. including foundations) and that the materials are sourced locally and/or from a sustainable source.

Mat 3 - Responsible sourcing of materials, finishing elements – as above, but apply to joinery, fitted furniture and finishings.

Mat 4 – Recycling – points for the provision of internal and/or external storage space for recyclable materials.

WATER – 10 POINTS

Wat 1 – Internal potable water use – points for limiting the amount of potable or mains water used in the house. From 142 litres per person, per day with points increasing to 88 litres per person, per day. There is an issue here with definitions as the standard measures 'bedspaces' rather than people. As the assessment is done from drawings and specifications, if the drawings show four double bedrooms, that will be counted as eight bedspaces, irrespective of the number of people in occupation. Theoretically, the more bedspaces designed into the house the more water the people in occupation get to use.

Wat 2 – External potable water use – points for installing a rainwater collection system, where water is for external use only. This can be from a water butt to a rainwater harvesting system.

LAND USE AND ECOLOGY – 12 POINTS

Eco 1 – Ecological value of site – points for building on a brown-field site.

Eco 2 – Ecological enhancement – points for having an ecologist report on how best to improve the site and implementing those suggestions

Eco 3 – Ecological protection – points for using the same ecologist to highlight the ecological features of the site (trees, hedges, streams, ponds, etc) and the steps to be taken to ensure they remain in the same state at the end of the project.

Eco 4 – Change of ecological value of site – points for increasing the number of species of flora and fauna living (or able to live) on the site.

Eco 5 – Building footprint – this relates to the ratio of the floor area of the building to its footprint. That is a house with a floor area of 200m2 with a ground floor (and thereby footprint) of 100m^2 will have a ration of 2:1. Points are awarded for ratios of 2.5:1 to 3.5:1

HEALTH AND WELL BEING – 14 POINTS

Hea 1 – Daylighting – points for ensuring that circulation rooms (kitchen, living room, etc) have good daylight and a view of the sky.

Hea 2 – Sound insulation – (half the marks available in this section are awarded for good sound insulation, recognising that noise is the most upsetting of pollutants). Points are awarded for testing that demonstrates that the requirements of Building Regulations Part E have been exceeded.

Hea 3 – Private Space – points for the provision of private outside space, such as a garden.

As can be seen, the Ecohomes standard covers all the main points of a sustainable build. It can be argued, with some justification, that some of the standards need a bit of re-consideration; water use would be a case in point. But if nothing else, Ecohomes provides a yardstick that the sustainable self-builder can measure their design by. You also get a pretty certificate with sunflowers on it to hang in the hall.

7

5. A PRÉCIS OF THE CODE FOR SUSTAINABLE HOMES

A complete version of the Code is downloadable from www.breeam.org

From April 2007, the Code for Sustainable Homes replaced Ecohomes for new housing in England. Ecohomes continues to be used for refurbished housing in England and for all housing in Scotland and Wales.

The code goes a step further than Ecohomes in setting out minimum standards for six main aspects of the property and the construction process.

- **Energy efficiency /CO$_2$**
- **Water efficiency**
- **Surface water management**
- **Site waste management**
- **Household waste management**
- **Use of materials**

The code steps-up on Ecohomes in a number of ways: it introduces minimum standards for energy and water efficiency at every level, it uses a simpler system of awarding points, with the weighting system removed, it introduces new areas of sustainability, such as Lifetime Homes and composting facilities.

The code currently sits alongside Ecohomes and the planning system and is set to become an intrinsic part of planning and building regulation compliance control.

The code uses a sustainability rating system – indicated by stars, to rate the overall sustainability performance of a home. A rating of one ★ to six ★★★★★★ is available. One star ★ is the entry level – around 10 percent above the level of the Building Regulations – and six stars ★★★★★★ is the highest level – reflecting excellent performance in sustainability terms and specifically zero carbon emissions.

The following is an extract from the code technical guidance.

MINIMUM STANDARDS

7

Code level	Category	Minimum Standard
	Energy/CO$_2$	
1(★)	Percentage improvement over	10%
2(★★)	Target Emission Rate (TRE)	18%
3(★★★)	as determined by the	25%
4(★★★★)	2006 Building Regulation	44%
5(★★★★★)	Standards	100%
6(★★★★★★)		**A 'zero carbon home' (heating, lighting, hot water and all other energy uses in the home)**
	Water	
1(★)	internal potable water	**120 l/p/d**
2(★★)	consumption measured in	**120 l/p/d**
3(★★★)	litres per person per day(l/p/d)	**105 l/p/d**
4(★★★★)		**105 l/p/d**
5(★★★★★)		**80 l/p/d**
6(★★★★★★)		**80 l/p/d**
	Materials	
1(★)	Environmental impact of materials†	At least three of the following 5 key element of construction are specified to achieve a BRE Green Guide 2006 rating of at least – Roof structure and finishes – External walls – Upper floor – Internal walls – Windows and doors
	Surface Water Run-off	
1(★)	Surface water management	Ensure that peak run-off rates and annual volumes of run-off will be no greater than the previous conditions for the development site

† A probable future development regarding the environmental impact of materials is to reward resource efficiency, as well as the use of resources that are more sustainable, by developing "Ecopoints per m^2" as a measure for this item. However, it may be that the 'Green Guide' route will remain as a simple route for smaller developments.

7

It can be seen that the code moves the game on from Ecohomes. As an example, a one ★ rating for water use requires a usage of not more than 120 litres per person per day (l/p/d), falling to 80 l/p/d at 6 ★. Ecohomes starts at 142 l/p/d and falls to 88 l/p/d. The minimum standard for surface water is '...no greater than the previous conditions for the development site.' This effectively means that rain water from the roof and driveways have to be contained on site rather than discharged into main drains. The thinking is that these minimum levels will be moved up over time encouraging (or forcing) us to achieve higher levels of sustainability and making ever more use of renewable energy.

Clearly the legislation is a bit of a muddle at the moment with three different instruments to deal with, each vying for contention – Building Regs, Ecohomes and the code. The code (and to an extent Ecohomes) requires energy performance around 10 percent better than Part L. The Government has suggested that these will be ratcheted-up to 25 percent in 2010, 44 percent in 2013 and zero carbon in 2016. It can be argued that Parts C, F and L of the Building Regs, the instrument we have grown to know and love, is valueless if the Code for Sustainable Homes, or Ecohomes, is the standard we actually need to adopt. I guess they will sort it out one day.

The good news for us, the people who just want to build one sustainable house, is that if Bovis, Wimpey, Barratts et al are compelled to build sustainable houses the existing, largely cottage, industry that supplies sustainable materials will need to grow dramatically. Big players will get involved in a burgeoning market and bring all the benefits of scale and accessibility. We will not have to spend 10 hours on the internet looking for sustainable roof tiles because the local builders' merchant will be stocking them.

INDEX

8

8

8